LOSE
THE
WEIGHT
OF THE
WORLD

LOSE
THE
WEIGHT
OF THE
WORLD

LOSE
THE
WEIGHT
OF THE
WORLD

DR. CHARLES E. BLAIR
AND JUDY STONECIPHER

New Leaf Press

First printing: July 1997

ISBN: 0-89221-346-9
Library of Congress Catalog Number: 97-65168

Cover design by Steve Diggs & Friends, Nashville

TABLE OF CONTENTS

FORWARD

In case you think you have just spotted a major spelling error in the title on this page, relax. You haven't. We deliberately chose to head this section Forward rather than the more common Foreword after a quick trip through the "f" section of the dictionary.

You see, we discovered that the definition of *Foreword* consisted of a rather illusive, one-word description: *"preface."* So we flipped to the "p" section where we discovered that a preface is *a written introduction to a book intended to elucidate the text to follow.* Huh?

It didn't take long to decide that the folks reading this book probably did not want to be elucidated. Therefore, they probably didn't need a pre-face. But what we all need and what we all want is an occasional about-face. Change. Progressive, radical, onward advancing towards improvement or progress. Which, by the way, is the definition of Forward, and the reason we chose it.

And while we can't guarantee that you won't find a misspelling elsewhere in the book, we can guarantee that the title on this page is not a mistake. The only mistake connected with this page will be the one you make if you stop reading here and fail to shed the weight God never intended for you to bear.

But if you continue forward through the pages of this

book, we can promise you progressive, radical, onward advancing towards improvement in your walk with Him.

—The Authors

One thing I do,
forgetting those things which are behind
and reaching forward to those things which are ahead I
press toward the goal for the prize
of the upward call of God in Christ Jesus.
— Philippians 3:13,14

INTRODUCTION

After the holidays (and several times throughout the year after that!) nearly everyone has a pound or two . . . a roll here . . . an inch there . . . they'd like to shed or at least tone up.

Interestingly, even Scripture affirms the importance of physical fitness. But *spiritual* fitness is just as important; actually, more important.

Yet, too many times after salvation, we Christians pick up weight. The first "pound" or two goes relatively unnoticed. But left unchecked, one pound leads to five. And before long, if we're not careful, we become spiritually overweight, burdened down with problems and concerns that leave us sluggish at best, ineffective and lethargic at worst.

Hundreds of Christians were surveyed in preparation for this book. They were asked what they thought were the top ten "weights" (problems, concerns, burdens, fears, anxieties) hindering Christians in America today.

We were surprised at some of their answers. You may be, too. But chances are, you or someone you know is struggling right now with a spiritual "weight" problem.

But there is hope and there is help for all who are disciplined enough to find and follow *Lose the Weight of the World.*

This book is set up in triplets, three chapters per topic,

followed by a five-day scriptural diet and exercise plan. It begins with some rather unusual verses and with some rather unusual objects.

So put on your sweats, grab your Bible, and prepare to begin the most rigorous spiritual workout you've ever had.

Let us lay aside every weight . . .
and let us run with endurance the race that
is set before us.
— Hebrews 12:1

PART 1
OVERWEIGHT OR UNDERWEIGHT?

1

BE A PRINCE

But you are a chosen generation, a royal priesthood,
a holy nation, His own special people,
that you may proclaim the praises
of Him who called you out of darkness
into His marvelous light.
— 1 Peter 2:9

There are a couple of interesting verses found in the Book of Proverbs, the book written by the wise man Solomon:

Dishonest scales are an abomination to the Lord, But a just weight is His delight (Prov. 11:1).

Divers weights and divers measures, They are both alike, an abomination to the Lord (Prov. 20:10).

Keeping those verses in mind, consider Numbers 7. The opening verses of that chapter tell us that the tabernacle had just been completed and set up. Moses had anointed and consecrated it, and the 12 priests of the 12 tribes of Israel began bringing offerings. Their offerings consisted of sacrifices, of course; but also of *vessels* to be used in the tabernacle for the service of the Lord.

Offhand you may not know it, but Numbers 7 is a rather lengthy chapter — 89 verses to be exact. The reason it's so long is because each of those 12 prince's gifts is detailed within the chapter.

First the prince of Judah came. And he brought vessels:
(1) silver platter, 130 shekels in weight
(1) silver bowl, 70 shekels in weight
(1) gold spoon, 10 shekels in weight (Num. 7:13-14).
Then the prince of Issachar came with his offering of vessels:
(1) silver platter, 130 shekels in weight
(1) silver bowl, 70 shekels in weight
(1) gold spoon, 10 shekels in weight (Num. 7:19-20).
Next the prince of Zebulun came bringing his offering:
(1) silver platter, 130 shekels in weight
(1) silver bowl, 70 shekels in weight
(1) gold spoon, 10 shekels in weight (Num. 7:25-26).
Then the prince of Reuben, the prince of Simeon, and the prince of Gad, each one bringing . . .
(1) silver platter, 130 shekels
(1) silver bowl, 70 shekels
(1) gold spoon, 10 shekels! (Num. 7:31-32; 37-38; 43-44).
One by one the other six came, the princes of Ephraim, Manasseh, Benjamin, Dan, Asher, and Naphtali, each one bringing — you guessed it —
(1) silver platter, 130 shekels
(1) silver bowl, 70 shekels
(1) gold spoon, 10 shekels! (Num. 7:49-50; 55-56; 61-62; 67-68; 73-74; 79-80).

> This was the dedication offering for the altar from the leaders of Israel, when it was anointed: twelve silver platters, twelve silver bowls, and twelve gold pans. Each silver platter

weighed one hundred and thirty shekels and each bowl seventy shekels. All the silver of the vessels weighed two thousand four hundred shekels, according to the shekel of the sanctuary. The twelve gold pans full of incense weighed ten shekels apiece, according to the shekel of the sanctuary; all the gold of the pans weighed one hundred and twenty shekels" (Num. 7:84-86).

Each gift was identical — right down to the weight of the spoons! There was not one vessel that was a diverse, or *different,* weight. And the measurement was "according to the shekel of the sanctuary."

Back in Leviticus 27:25, under the Law, God had said, "And all your valuations shall be according to the shekel of the sanctuary: twenty gerahs to the shekel." You see, this business of weight was a *serious* matter with the Lord.

And when it came to the vessels used in the *service* of the Lord, weight became a *sacred* matter. And that shouldn't surprise us. God is the same yesterday, today, and forever. He's a God of order and exactness.

Scripture tells us that when it came to creation, He "establish[ed] a weight for the wind, And apportion[ed] the waters by measure" (Job 28:25).

Isaiah said the following about God:

Who has measured the waters in the hollow of His hand, measured heaven with a span, and calculated the dust of the earth in a measure? Weighed the mountains in scales and the hills in a balance (Isa. 40:12).

When God gave Noah the directions for the ark, and when He gave Moses the pattern for the tabernacle, He gave those directions cubit by cubit by cubit.

As David collected the materials for the temple he gave the following instructions: 1 Chronicles 28 records the following about David. . . .

He gave gold by weight for things of gold
. . . silver by weight . . . for the lampstands . . .
and their lamps of gold, by weight . . . for the
lampstands of silver by weight. . . . And by weight
he gave gold for the tables . . . and silver for the
tables of silver . . . he gave gold by weight for
every bowl; and . . . silver by weight for every
bowl and refined gold by weight for the altar of
incense (1 Chron. 28:14-18).

Why? Because, David said in verse 19,

All this . . . the Lord made me understand in
writing, by His hand upon me, all the works of
these plans.

What was true for the tabernacle was true for the
temple. The gold and silver vessels were prepared according to weight. They were not to be too light and not too
heavy, but just right: fit and durable for a lifetime of service.

But now there is no tabernacle. There is no temple,
and there are no carefully weighed gold or silver vessels.
Instead, according to Scripture, *we* are the vessels God uses
in His service.

What if God, wanting to show His wrath and
to make His power known, endured with much
long-suffering the vessels of wrath prepared for
destruction, and that He might make known the
riches of His glory on the vessels of mercy, which
He had prepared beforehand for glory, even us
whom He called (Rom. 9:22-24).

But we have this treasure in earthen vessels,
that the excellence of the power may be of God
and not of us (2 Cor. 4:7).

But in a great house there are not only vessels of gold and silver, but also of wood and clay, some for honor and some for dishonor. There- fore, if anyone cleanses himself from the latter, he will be a vessel for honor, sanctified and use- ful for the Master, prepared for every good work (2 Tim. 2:20-21).

Just as those tabernacle and temple vessels were mea- sured and weighed, *we* are measured and weighed. Just as there was a prescribed weight for those vessels, there is a prescribed, optimal weight — a standard of *spiritual* fit- ness — for *us* as vessels of the Lord. We're not to be too light, or lacking things God wants us to have; and we're not to be too heavy, encumbered with things God wants us to shed. We're to be spiritually fit for a lifetime of fellow- ship and service with Him.

Job said,

Does He not see my ways, And count all my steps? If I have walked with falsehood, Or if my foot has hastened to deceit, Let me be weighed on honest scales, That God may know my integ- rity (Job 31:4-6).

And Isaiah said, "The way of the just is uprightness; O Most Upright, You weigh the path of the just" (Isa. 26:7).

As Isaiah well knew, that path is not a sandy beach beside a quiet sea. It's not a flower-strewn walkway through life. It's a race track according to Hebrews 12:1. And it's already set before us. But the question is, are you in shape to run it?

Let us lay aside every weight . . .
and let us run with endurance
the race that is set before us.
— Hebrews 12:1

2

HOW BIG IS YOUR BOWL?

But reject profane and old wives' fables,
and exercise yourself rather to godliness.
For bodily exercise profits a little,
but godliness is profitable for all things,
having promise of the life that now is
and of that which is to come.
This is a faithful saying and worthy of all acceptance.
— 1 Timothy 4:7-9

Over the past decade, physical fitness has become a major emphasis in America, and it's never more obvious than during the holiday season. No sooner have we pushed away from the turkey and trimmings at Thanksgiving, than the commercials for the health clubs and weight loss plans begin, each assuring us that we still have time to be just the right weight — toned up, firmed up — for the Christmas season.

And then it's as if someone out there in media-land is watching, and as soon as we've popped the last piece of fudge in our mouths Christmas night, the commercials begin rolling again, spelling out the New Year's resolution they think we all need to make.

But really, no one has to tell us we need to be physically fit. And no one has to tell us that most of us are *not* physically fit.

Best-selling author Covert Bailey says:

> Probably 90 percent of the public knows that they SHOULD exercise. If you ask people on the street if exercise is as good as it's cracked up to be, most will say yes. All of them know that it helps to control weight, and most people can list a dozen other benefits. Those who used to exercise will tell you that when they did, they felt better, slept better, and were less tense, and they wish they could get started again.[1]

But this thing called "physical fitness" is more than something most of us have on our wish lists. It's even more than big business at holiday time. It's a science, with degreed career specialists in both the public and private sectors.

These professional fitness specialists all operate within the parameters of well-defined guidelines, guidelines established by such prestigious national organizations as the American Medical Association, the President's Council on Physical Fitness and Sports, and the American College of Sports Medicine.

There are no diverse (different) weights and measurements. The tables used in New York City are the same ones used in Muleshoe, Texas. And unfortunately for some of us, these fitness experts don't use dishonest scales. They use the same one the doctor uses — not that personal, *adjustable* bathroom scale we all keep at home!

When you go to see one of these fitness specialists, the first thing they do is assess you. That assessment is not based on whether they like you or not. That assessment is not based on how you, or they, think your clothes fit. And they sure don't assess you by how you feel when you're sitting comfortably at home watching their commercials!

The fitness assessment is done by the book. By the charts. By the tables. By the graphs. They check your pulse rate, not while you're sitting in front of the TV eating popcorn, but when you're in front of them, on a treadmill, sweating!

They judge you by standards that *you* didn't — and probably wouldn't — select. They evaluate you by standards that you didn't set, but that somebody else set for your good. And then they design a program — diet, exercise, rest — to bring you in line with those prescribed standards.

If the scale says your "bowl" is lighter than 70 shekels, then the standard says you're *under*weight; and the fitness specialist spells out what you're lacking and what you need to do to gain *what* you need *where* you need it. If your "platter" is heavier than 130 shekels, then the chart says you're *over*weight; and the fitness specialist spells out how to lose *what* and *where.*

But maybe your bowl is right on target. So is your platter. Even your spoon falls right on the money at 10 shekels. You're smack-dab where you ought to be on the height/weight/age charts. However, it's been years since you touched your toes (unless *they* came up real close to your hands). And when it came to the treadmill, you were sure they called it a *dead*-mill and you just about complied right around lap two!

You see, just because you *look* slim and trim doesn't necessarily mean you're physically fit. You can fall within the guidelines of the height/weight/age chart, but lack the heart and muscle tone, the flexibility and the stamina, to meet the other standards.

By definition, when you're physically fit, you possess certain measurable physical attributes. By application, when you're physically fit, you reflect "the ability to work with vigor and pleasure without undue fatigue, with energy left for enjoying hobbies and recreational activities, and for meeting unforeseen emergencies. It relates to how you feel mentally as well as physically."[2]

Likewise, *spiritual* fitness can be viewed as a measure of a person's *spiritual* strength, stamina, and flexibility. Spiritual fitness reflects your ability to work (minister, serve) with vigor and pleasure without undue fatigue, with energy left over for enjoying life, and for meeting unforeseen emergencies.

Isaiah said it well many centuries ago:

> But those who wait on the Lord shall renew their strength; They shall mount up with wings like eagles, They shall run, and not be weary, They shall walk, and not faint (Isa. 40:31).

It becomes obvious that each of us needs a personal *spiritual* fitness specialist even more than we need a personal *physical* fitness specialist. And fortunately, we already have the most balanced, personalized, well-integrated spiritual fitness diet and exercise program with guaranteed results — free of charge! It's found in the sacred Scriptures. And God himself has already agreed to be your own personal spiritual fitness counselor!

His program is not something new or trendy. It's been tested and has worked through the centuries for people in all walks of life everywhere on earth; from slaves to kings; men, women, youth, children; for the childless, the childish, and the childlike; in good times, bad times, sad times, and absolutely mad times.

What's true of *physical* fitness is also true of *spiritual* fitness. Being spiritually fit is more than looking or trying to act spiritually fit. When you're *spiritually* fit, you fall within the unchanging, specified, measurable parameters contained in the Word of God.

With spiritual fitness, there are no diverse weights or measurements. God doesn't use a dishonest scale. The tables

He uses now are the same as He used for Abraham, for David, and for Paul. The standards are no easier for you. But they're no harder, either.

Your preacher didn't make up the spiritual fitness charts; *God* did. Your preacher can't alter the tables or slow down the treadmill, and neither can you.

Proverbs 16:2 says, "All the ways of a man are pure in his own eyes, But the Lord weighs the spirits."

God set the standards, and He set them for our good. His goal, according to Hebrews 12:1 is to *get* us in shape and *keep* us in shape to run — and win — the race that He has set before us. Now the question is, how big is *your* bowl?

Let us lay aside every weight . . . and let us run with endurance the race that is set before us.
— Hebrews 12:1

Endnotes

[1]Covert Bailey, *The New Fit or Fat* (Boston, MA: Houghton Mifflin Company, 1991), p. 6.

[2]Philip E. Allsen, Joyce M. Harrison, and Barbara Vance, *Fitness for Life, an Individualized Approach* (Dubuque, IA: Wm. C. Brown Publishers, 1984), p. 5.

3

DO YOU *REALLY* WANT TO KNOW?

But let a man examine himself.
— 1 Corinthians 11:28

*Examine yourselves as towhether you
are in the faith. Prove yourselves.
Do you not know yourselves, that
Jesus Christ is in you? —
unless indeed you are disqualified.*
— 2 Corinthians 13:58

hen the writer of the Book of Hebrews penned the words now known as chapter 12, verse 1, he had in mind the Olympic games. Athletes trained for the events by running with weights strapped to their bodies. But when it came time for the actual race, those weights were hurled aside and left behind in the dust. That's the same kind of unhindered life the writer of Hebrews is encouraging believers to seize:

Let us lay aside every weight, and let us run with endurance the race that is set before us (Heb. 12:1).

23

The writer knew that the Christian race is no sprint. The Greek word translated *race* in Hebrews 12:1 is *agonia*. We get our word *agony* from the same root word. The race is tough. You can't be an *under*weight weakling and expect to complete it. Neither can you be an *over*weight blimp and expect to win it.

So the question is, how's your *race* weight? If you stepped with Job on God's *honest* scales, what would *your* spiritual weight be?

Belshazzar, king of Babylon, unwittingly stumbled onto God's scales one fateful night in a crowded banquet hall. As he praised the gods of gold and silver, the fingers of God penned his poundage on the wall for a thousand of his lords to read:

> Tekel: You have been weighed in the balances, and found wanting (Dan. 5:27).

Belshazzar was a spiritual underweight. That's probably no surprise. What more can anyone expect from a proud, idolatrous, potentate drunk with the power of an inherited heathen kingdom?

But certainly we should be able to expect more from religious leaders, right? After all, they are the caretakers of *God's* kingdom.

Unfortunately, when Jesus began His ministry, He discovered that both the professional religious leaders (the scribes), and the lay leaders (the Pharisees), were spiritually underweight weaklings. Not only were they incapable of running the race, they didn't even remember where the racetrack was!

> Woe to you, scribes and Pharisees, hypocrites! For you pay tithe of mint and anise and cumin, and have neglected the weightier matters of the law: justice and mercy and faith. These you ought to have done, without leaving the others undone (Matt. 23:23).

This religious bunch needed to gain some weight. They needed to pick up pounds of justice and mercy and faith. They lacked the weightier matters God intends for His people to have.

And who can forget the rich young ruler? You remember that he had kept all the laws from his youth. But Jesus looked at him — lovingly, the Scripture says — but told him he was a spiritual underweight. "One thing you lack," Jesus said.

But Jesus never pointed out a problem without providing a solution. This time was no different. Jesus told the young man he was spiritually unfit. But Jesus also designed a personal spiritual fitness program for him. It's recorded in Mark 10:21.

The first step was a warm-up walk. "Go your way," Jesus said. Step two involved some full-body exercises — holding a garage sale or carrying everything he owned to the market — for Jesus said, "Sell whatever you have." If you've ever had a garage sale or taken a truckload of merchandise to the flea market, you know how much exercise Jesus intended for the young man to get!

That exercise was to be followed by more walking — this time on a benevolence mission to the poor part of town. It also involved some upper body movement, reaching into his wallet and passing out to the poor.

The final step, the most grueling in this divinely designed fitness program, was a rigorous weight-lifting regimen. "Take up the cross, and follow Me," Jesus instructed.

And what were the rewards promised in exchange for spiritual fitness? "Treasure in heaven." A completed race. A prize at the finish line.

But only those who choose to be the right weight receive the rewards. Not the underweight. But not the *over-*weight either.

Martha of Bethany was overweight. Jesus showed up in the village one day, and Martha offered Him accommodations at her home. Martha, however, was so intent on pleasing the Lord that she became "cumbered about much serving" (Luke 10:40;KJV).

Jesus gently admonished her to shape up — shed the weight of worry and concern — by spending time sitting at His feet and hearing His Word.

We all know that even the best-intentioned people gain weight physically. So it really shouldn't be any surprise that even the best-intentioned people of God gain weight spiritually.

Even the chosen, the called, and the anointed of God must constantly guard against picking up unwanted weight. Mary loved the Lord. She wanted to serve Him the best meal He had ever eaten. But her good intentions led to spiritual weight gain.

Saul is another good example. This handsome young man from the tribe of Benjamin was chosen by God to become the first king of Israel. At first, Saul was so scared by the awesome responsibility God had placed upon him, that he hid. But in just a few short years, he picked up weight — pride . . . independence . . . disobedience — until he became unusable as an anointed vessel of God:

> So Samuel said, "When you were little in your own eyes, were you not head of the tribes of Israel? And did not the Lord anoint you king over Israel? . . . Has the Lord as great delight in burnt offerings and sacrifices, as in obeying the voice of the Lord ? Behold, to obey is better than sacrifice, and to heed than the fat of rams. For rebellion is as the sin of witchcraft, and stubbornness is as iniquity and idolatry. Because you have rejected the word of the Lord, He also has rejected you from being king" (1 Sam. 15:17-23).

Saul was so spiritually unfit and flabby that he was knocked out of the race altogether.

And then there was Peter. Poor Peter. Physically speaking, Peter was probably one of the most fit men of the 12 disciples chosen by the Lord. He had been a seasoned fishermen, slinging nets, rowing boats, hauling tons of fish to market.

Spiritually speaking, Peter had his moments. But one of his worst was out on the sea he knew so well. It happened one evening when Jesus came walking across the water toward the boat. Jesus spoke, and Peter stepped out on the waves to meet Him.

But shortly thereafter, Peter picked up weight — fear and doubt. His faith faltered, his goal faded from sight; and poor, overweight Peter began to sink. Fortunately, Peter cried out to the only One who could help him lose the spiritual weight he'd gained (Matt. 14:25-33).

NOW, WHAT ABOUT YOU?

Belshazzar, the scribes and Pharisees, the rich young ruler, Saul, Martha, Peter — they're all gone. They've run the race. And now the baton has passed to you, and it's time to step on the scale.

Most of us hate to step on the scale, particularly an *honest* scale, one that reveals our true weight loud and clear. But remember what Job said? Job *asked* God to weigh him — on *honest* scales (Job 31:6)!

DO YOU HAVE THAT KIND OF COURAGE?

Test it right now by responding to these two challenges: First of all, ask yourself, "Do I really want to know how I measure up, not by *my* standards, but by *His*?

Remember, Proverbs 16:2 says, "All the ways of a man are pure in his own eyes, But the Lord weighs the spirits."

You may think you're in pretty good shape, spiritually speaking. And maybe you are. But maybe you're not. Maybe you're *under*weight, lacking some of the things God wants or expects you to have. But do you *really* want to know?

Maybe you're *over*weight, encumbered with things God wants and expects you to shed or at least tone up. But do you *really* want to know?

And secondly, are you *really ready* to do something about it?

Are you really ready to go to work and exercise the discipline it will take to gain what you lack, or lose what you must?

The rich young ruler really wanted to know how he measured up, spiritually speaking. He asked to be assessed by the Master of spiritual fitness. The rich young ruler willingly stepped on the scale, and Jesus told him exactly what he needed to do.

But the rich young ruler wasn't *really ready* to do anything about it.

Peter, on the other hand, cried out for help as soon as he picked up that extra weight and began to sink. And the Lord reached out, lifted one spiritually overweight fisherman out of the waves, and used him as an honored vessel for the rest of his life.

God is ready to do that for you too, right now, but only if *you're* really ready.

DO YOU REALLY WANT TO KNOW HOW YOU MEASURE UP?

And when you find out, are you really ready to do something about it? If so, tell your Heavenly Father right now. Make a commitment to Him and to yourself. That commitment might be something like this:

> *Father,*
> *I want to be a vessel of honor*
>   *that you can bless and use.*
> *I'm ready to step on your honest scale*
>   *to find out how I really measure up.*

And Lord,
> *I know that the things I find out*
> > *may be hard —*
> *the things I need to gain*
> > *may be difficult to develop;*
> *and the things I need to lose*
> > *may be even harder to get rid of.*

But I'm ready.
I'm ready, by Your grace,
> *to do something about*
> *my spiritual weight.*
> > *In Jesus' holy Name I pray,*
> > *Amen.*

PART 1
SPIRITUAL HEALTH AND FITNESS EVALUATION

To begin this program, it is important to complete the following spiritual health and fitness evaluation over the next several days. Be sure to answer each question prayerfully and honestly.

A spiritual diet plan (1 Pet. 2:2) and exercise program (1 Tim. 4:7) for each day is also included.

DAY 1

TODAY'S DIET: Read Eph. 4:11-16 and 2 Peter 3:18.
EXERCISE: Just as there is a close correlation between *physical* age, height, and weight, there is also a close correlation between *spiritual* age, height, and weight. As you begin assessing your spiritual weight, seeking to determine whether you are *under*weight, *over*weight, or *just about the right weight,* be sure to consider your spiritual age. Remember that God never expects the same level of spiritual maturity from a new Christian as He does from one who's known the Lord many years. But He does expect us to grow!

• Complete the following survey:
1. How long have you been a Christian? _____
2. How much do you feel you have grown in the Lord?
   ❑ little   ❑ some   ❑ much
3. Think of a difficult situation you faced recently. How did you handle it?
   ❑ about the same way you would have before you were a Christian.
   ❑ about the same way you would have shortly after becoming a Christian.
   ❑ differently; more mature, more Christ-like.

• Think about your responses. Discuss them in prayer with the Lord, seeking His counsel about the growth you want to achieve.

DAY 2

TODAY'S DIET: Read Matthew 23:23 and Mark 10:17-22.

EXERCISE: The Pharisees and the rich young ruler were devout and law-abiding, yet they were *under*weight spiritual weaklings. They thought they knew and kept the Scriptures. How well do you know the Scriptures?

1. When the pastor asks us to turn to a Scripture passage, most of the time,
   - ❏ I don't even know where the book is located in my Bible.
   - ❏ I know the general location of the book and can find it relatively easily.
   - ❏ I can find the passage quickly and easily.

2. In the past year
   - ❏ I have memorized no new Scriptures.
   - ❏ I have memorized a few new Scriptures.
   - ❏ I have followed a systematic Scripture memorization plan.

3. In the past year
   - ❏ I have rarely read my Bible between Sundays.
   - ❏ I sometimes read my Bible between Sundays.
   - ❏ I always read my Bible at least once between Sundays.
   - ❏ I have followed a systematic Bible reading plan.

• Think about your responses. Discuss them in prayer with the Lord. Compare your devotion with that of the religious rulers you read about. Where did they fail? Where are you failing?

DAY 3

TODAY'S DIET: Read 1 Thessalonians 4:1-12.

EXERCISE: Consider your responses on Days 1 and 2. Are you *under*weight in any areas? God's desire as expressed by Paul in the verses you read is that you "lack nothing" (verse 12). Ask the Lord to weigh you today on His honest scale (Job 31:6) and reveal to you anything you may be lacking. Make a note of it here and commit its acquisition to the Lord.

_____

_____

_____

DAY 4

TODAY'S DIET: Read James 2:1-6 and 2 Peter 1:1-9.
EXERCISE: Jesus repeatedly told the religious leaders of His day that they were blind as to their own spiritual condition. Proverbs 16:2 says,

> All the ways of a man are pure in his own
> eyes, But the Lord weighs the spirits.

Ask the Lord to show you areas where *you* may still be blind to your own spiritual condition. Select one of the "underweight" areas you found in your previous days of evaluation. Take a few minutes today to actively build up that weak area — begin memorizing a new Scripture, for instance.

DAY 5

TODAY'S DIET: Read Luke 10:38-42.
EXERCISE: Martha loved the Lord very much but was still spiritually overweight. And you may be, too. When you think about serving the Lord —going to church, teaching a class, etc. — what kinds of things come to your mind first — the details involved, or the joy you experience?

• Review your previous days' answers regarding things you lack spiritually — an effective prayer life . . . Bible study program . . . Scripture memorization . . . and so on.

• List the things that keep you from achieving victory in those areas. Be honest!

_____

_____

_____

• These things are weights! They are the things *you* are worried and troubled about. They are the things God wants and expects you to lay aside in order to run the race He has set before you! Begin to commit these things to Him and claim victory in the weeks ahead!

P.S. Perhaps you discovered this week that you are neither underweight or overweight; you're just about the right spiritual weight. But stay tuned. The next step is a look at your spiritual flexibility, strength, and stamina!

4

GOD DOESN'T USE TUPPERWARE

*But in a great house there are not only
vessels of gold and silver,
but also of wood and clay,
some for honor and some for dishonor.*
— 2 Timothy 2:20

Previously we looked at two verses in Proverbs and at a chapter in the Old Testament having to do with the weights of the vessels used in the service of the Lord in the tabernacle. You'll remember that each silver platter, each silver bowl, and each gold spoon offered by the 12 princes of the 12 tribes of Israel was identical in weight.

God had said in His Word,

Divers [various] weights are an abomination
to the Lord (Prov. 20:10).

But a just weight is His delight (Prov. 11:1).

You also probably remember that those principles were carried forward to the time of the temple, when *its* gold and silver vessels were also prepared according by *weight for the work of the Lord.*

Those gold and silver vessels were important. And

there were prescribed standards for each of them. Standards for weight, yes; but also standards for composition . . . durability . . . strength. Gold and silver were the *precious* materials of the day. And they were the *durable* materials of the day.

There was no dishwasher-safe, microwaveable, stain resistant, chip resistant, child-, pet- and husband-proof plastic or stainless steel. No Revereware . . . no Farberware . . . no Corning Ware. And this may come as a real shock to you, but even King Solomon — with all his wisdom, with all his wealth, with all his resources and foreign contacts — did not have a single piece of Tupperware!

The durable vessels of *that* day were the vessels of gold and silver more durable than the animal skins that held the water and the wine. They were more durable than the pottery that cracked and broke.

So the vessels of the temple were prepared for *a lifetime of service . . . by weight . . .* of gold and silver — the precious, strong, more durable materials of the day.

But now, there is no tabernacle. There is no temple; and no carefully weighed, durably forged gold or silver vessels. Furthermore, God doesn't use Tupperware in His service. Instead, He uses vessels made of clay — people. Vessels that He himself molds, cleanses with the blood of His Son, selects for specific service, and uses for His glory.

> But we have this treasure in earthen vessels, that the excellence of the power may be of God and not of us (2 Cor. 4:7).

> Does not the potter have power over the clay, from the same lump to make one vessel for honor and another for dishonor? What if God, wanting to show His wrath and to make His power known, endured with much long-suffering the vessels of wrath prepared for destruction, and that He might make known the riches of His glory on the ves-

sels of mercy, which He had prepared beforehand for glory, even us whom He called, not of the Jews only, but also of the Gentiles? (Rom. 9:21-24).

We are the vessels "for honor, sanctified and useful for the Master, prepared for every good work" (2 Tim. 2:21). God doesn't use Tupperware. Or Revereware or Farberware or Corning Ware. He uses Earthenware — people. But He needs them to be durable. If you're a Christian, you're a vessel. Now it's time to see just how strong — just how durable — you really are.

Let us lay aside every weight . . .
and let us run with endurance the race
that is set before us.
— Hebrews 12:1

5

IN IT FOR THE DURATION

I have fought the good fight,
I have finished the race, I have kept the faith.
Finally, there is laid up for me
the crown of righteousness,
which the Lord, the righteous Judge,
will give to me on that Day,
and not to me only
but also to all who have loved His appearing.
— 2 Timothy 4:7-8

Hopefully, you have already used the guidelines following chapter 3 to assess your spiritual weight as a vessel of the Lord. If you did, you fell in one of the three following categories:

1. Spiritually underweight. You lack some of the qualities, attributes, or habits that God wants and expects you to have.

2. Spiritually overweight. You are carrying some weights, cares, concerns, unprofitable habits, or problems that God wants you to shed or at least tone up.

3. Just about right. You are one of the fortunate few who are in pretty good spiritual shape,
at least, weight-wise.

But *spiritual* fitness is a lot like *physical* fitness. Just
because you *look* slim and trim doesn't necessarily mean
you're physically fit. You can fall smack-dab within the
guidelines of the height/weight/age chart, but lack the
strength, heart, and muscle tone to even lift a spoonful of
corn flakes to your mouth!

Paul said in our theme verse, "Let us lay aside every
weight *and* let us *run with endurance* the race that is set
before us" (Heb. 12:1). Yes, you have to be the right weight,
but this is a marathon. You're going to have to be *strong* —
durable — because *this* race is tough.

You're going to have to "*strive* to enter in
through the narrow gate" (Luke 13:24).

You're going to have to "*contend* earnestly
for the faith" (Jude 1:3). Lap after lap after lap . . .
mile after mile after mile.

You're in it for the duration, so you're going to have
to be durable; you're going to have to be strong.

Spiritual strength, or durability, is a historical, scriptural principle. It was the First Commandment of the Law
that God gave to Moses:

And you shall love the Lord your God with
all your heart, with all your soul, with all your
mind, and with all your *strength* (Mark 12:30).

And the last words of Moses spoken to the children of
Israel were nearly identical. Moses said,

I call heaven and earth as witnesses today
(Deut. 30:19).

Love the Lord your God with all your heart

and with all your soul (Deut. 30:6).

Be strong (Deut. 31:6).

It almost is ridiculous how may times those two little words, "be strong," are batted around in the next few chapters!

First Moses told the people to be strong; then he called Joshua aside and told him to be strong (Deut. 31:7, 23).

After Moses died, *God* called Joshua aside and said:

Joshua, be strong (Josh. 1:6).

Joshua, be strong (Josh. 1:7).

Have not I commanded you? BE STRONG! (Josh. 1:9).

Then the *people* met with Joshua and *they* said, "Joshua, be strong" (Josh. 1:18).

Then *Joshua* turned right around in chapter 10, verse 25, and said to the *people,* "Be strong."

Why the repetition?

Because the race to win ("Let us lay aside every weight . . . and let us run with endurance the race that is set before us") is a marathon. It's tough . . . it's hard. And you've gotta be strong.

As David turned the reigns of government over to his son, Solomon, David gave some fatherly and kingly advice. "Be strong," he said (1 Chron. 22:13).

When Sennacherib, the Assyrian king, threatened the people of God, King Hezekiah instituted martial law for the sole purpose of gathering the people together . . . to encourage them . . . to exhort them to be strong:

Then he [Hezekiah] set military captains over the people, gathered them together to him in the open square of the city gate, and gave them encouragement, saying, "Be strong" (2 Chron. 32:6-7).

God sent a heavenly messenger to Daniel as he was held captive in a foreign land, and the messenger said, "O man greatly beloved, fear not! Peace be to you; be strong, yes, be strong" (Dan. 10:19).

After God arrested Saul on the road to Damascus, He told Ananias to go and minister to Saul. "Go," the Lord said to Ananias, "for he is a chosen vessel of Mine to bear My name before Gentiles, kings, and the children of Israel. For I will show him how many things he must suffer for My name's sake" (Acts 9:15-16).

This one who would become the apostle Paul was going to have to be strong — to be durable — for the work God had called him to do. And faithful to the call, Paul insisted that others develop the same durability he, himself, had found so necessary and valuable.

To the church at Corinth Paul wrote, "Watch, stand fast in the faith . . . be strong" (1 Cor. 16:13).

To the church at Ephesus he wrote, "Finally, my brethren, be strong in the Lord, and in the power of his might" (Eph. 6:10).

And to Timothy, Paul said, "You therefore, my son, be strong" (2 Tim. 2:1).

God's command is clear — from Old Testament Law to New Testament church: Be strong. The next question is, How?

> *Let us lay aside every weight . . .*
> *and let us run with endurance*
> *the race that is set before us.*
> — Hebrews 12:1

6

DON'T MAKE
YOURSELF SICK!

Give to the Lord, O kindreds of the peoples,
Give to the Lord glory and strength.
— Psalm 96:7

Daniel the prophet said, "The people who know their God shall be strong, and carry out great exploits" (Dan. 11:32). They'll run the race, complete the race; they'll even win the race when it's all said and run.

BUT WHERE DOES THIS STRENGTH COME FROM?

And, if you're weak, how do you build up spiritual muscles?

If you're weak physically, the best way to build up physical muscles is by exercise. Work out. Walk. Ride a bike. Lift weights. Do aerobics. And the same is true of lagging, sagging spiritual muscles.

But God said,

Exercise yourself toward godliness" (1 Tim. 4:7).

> Be strong, all you people of the land . . . and work (Hag. 2:4).

Anyone who has followed a regimen of physical exercise for even a short length of time will tell you how energizing exercise is, how it helps you sleep better, think better, and how it builds strength and endurance.

And what's true of the physical is true of the spiritual — sadly, in more ways than one.

> In the physical realm, we're seeing a rise in "hypokinetic" disease — "disease that is related to, or caused by, a lack of regular physical activity[1]" — coronary heart disease, high blood pressure, lower back problems, increased body fat, and joint disorders.

Not only are we physically unfit, we're making ourselves sick! Why? Because more and more of us are failing to follow a regular exercise program, and, thanks to modern technology, even everyday chores require less and less of us physically.

Dishwashers have replaced dish washers, riding mowers have replaced push mowers, cars and elevators and escalators have replaced everyday walking; so, many of us — even some of us who are just about the right *weight* — are out of shape. We have weak muscles. We lack strength and durability.

> Although the human body is designed for movement and strenuous physical activity, exercise is rarely a part of the average individual's lifestyle. One cannot expect the human body to function optimally and to remain healthy for extended periods of time if it is abused or not used as intended.[2]

THE SAME IS TRUE SPIRITUALLY SPEAKING.

Here in 20th century America, Christendom has it pretty soft.

There are no Sauls banging on our doors, dragging us off to be stoned.

There are no Romans forcing us to fight wild animals in a bloodthirsty arena.

We don't have to walk miles to attend an underground church, or shiver in the cold under the cover of a wooded forest.

We don't have to hew the logs or build our churches. We don't even have to clean or repair them once we've bought them; we pay somebody else to do that.

We don't have to copy Scriptures by hand. We don't have to remember any words to a song; they're handed to us in a bulletin when we walk through the church door or they're projected on the wall for our convenient viewing.

There aren't many hungry to deliver food to. There are hospitals to take care of the sick, nursing homes to house the elderly.

We've slacked off exercising our prayer life, our Bible study.

We've forgotten the meaning and the blessing of the great hymns of the faith, we seldom make a call on the telephone, much less in person — and we, like everyone else, are weighed down with depression, stress, low self esteem, fear, and so on and on and on.

We're not only out of shape spiritually, we're making ourselves sick! We're suffering from *spiritual* hypokinetic disease, disease that is related to, or caused by, a lack of *regular spiritual activity.*

Just as our physical bodies were designed for movement and strenuous physical activity, so we as individual Christians, and corporately as the Church Body, were also designed for movement — for *strenuous* spiritual activity.

IT'S CALLED MINISTRY.

The command is clear: *Let us lay aside every weight . . . and let us run with endurance the race that is set before us. Be strong.*

Get fit. Stay fit. And maybe you are. But maybe you're not. How can you tell?

The wise man Solomon said, "If you faint in the day of adversity, your strength is small" (Prov. 24:10).

Maybe that's you. A towering pillar of jello when trouble strikes. Little strength. But don't give up. Having a little strength is a good beginning.

God said to the church at Philadelphia:

> I know your works. See, I have set before you an open door, and no one can shut it; for you have a little strength, have kept My word, and have not denied My name. . . . Behold, I am coming quickly! Hold fast what you have, that no one may take your crown (Rev. 3:8-11).

Maybe those verses are speaking to you. Maybe you have a little strength. You know the return of the Lord is near, you know that He has set before *you* an open door, and you'd like more strength to walk through that door . . . to run the race He's set before you.

There's a way. Just begin employing these six spiritual muscle-building exercises — six ways to help build your spiritual endurance, to help you to "be strong" — strong enough to run and finish the race that is set before us.

1. Be certain you have trusted Christ as your personal Saviour.

The psalmist wrote, "The Lord will give strength to *His* people" (Ps. 29:11).

God's promise of strength is not guaranteed to just anyone — only to those who have accepted the shed blood of God's sinless Son, the Lord Jesus Christ, as the only payment and the final payment for their sin.

For all have sinned and fall short of the glory of God (Rom. 3:23).

For the wages of sin is death, but the gift of God is eternal life in Christ Jesus our Lord (Rom. 6:23).

But God demonstrates His own love toward us, in that while we were still sinners, Christ died for us (Rom. 5:8).

That if you confess with your mouth the Lord Jesus and believe in your heart that God has raised Him from the dead, you will be saved. For with the heart one believes to righteousness, and with the mouth confession is made to salvation (Rom. 10:9-10).

2. Tone up your prayer life.

Seek the Lord and His strength; Seek His face evermore (Ps. 105:4).

But those who wait on the Lord shall renew their strength; they shall mount up with wings like eagles, they shall run and not be weary, they shall walk and not faint (Isa. 40:31).

3. Look for the bright side ... focus on the positive things God has done for you.

The joy of the Lord is your strength (Neh. 8:10).

The Lord is my strength and song (Ps. 118:14).

4. Read and obey God's Word, the Bible.

Therefore you shall keep every commandment which I command you today, that you may be strong (Deut. 11:8).

A wise man is strong, yes, a man of knowledge increases strength (Prov. 24:5).

5. Work. Get involved in local church ministry.

>Be strong, all you people of the land . . . and work (Hag. 2:4).

>Then Saul spent some days with the disciples at Damascus. Immediately he preached the Christ in the synagogues, that He is the Son of God. [And] Saul increased all the more in strength and confounded the Jews who dwelt in Damascus, proving that this Jesus is the Christ (Acts 9:19-22).

There is a direct tie between spiritual strength and personal involvement in Christ's church.

If you will receive Christ's vision for you, if you will seek first and foremost the building of His church, meeting the felt needs of others in Christ's name, making disciples, you will develop spiritual muscles. You'll grow strong in the Lord and in the power of His might (Eph. 6:10).

Let us lay aside every weight . . . and let us run with endurance the race that is set before us.
— Hebrews 12:1

Endnotes

[1]Philip E. Allsen, Joyce M. Harrison, and Barbara Vance, *Fitness for Life, an Individualized Approach* (Dubuque, IA: Wm. C. Brown Publishers, 1984), p. 4.

[2]Vivian H. Heyward, *Designs for Fitness, a Guide to Physical Fitness Appraisal and Exercise Prescription* (Minneapolis, MN: Burgess Publishing Company, 1984), p. 1.

PART 2
SPIRITUAL HEALTH AND FITNESS EVALUATION

To continue this program, it is important to complete the following spiritual health and fitness evaluation over the next several days. Be sure to answer each question prayerfully and honestly.

A spiritual diet plan (1 Pet. 2:2) and exercise program (1 Tim. 4:7) for each day is also included.

DAY 1

TODAY'S DIET: Read Mark 12:28-30, Hebrews 12:1 & Jude 1:4

EXERCISE: Step 1 of this program was to assess your *spiritual* weight. Perhaps as you did that, you found that you were *under*weight spiritually — that you lacked some of the things God wants and expects you to have. Perhaps you discovered you were *over*weight — that you are carrying some burdens . . . cares . . . concerns . . . habits . . . something, that by God's grace, you would like to shed . . . or at least tone up. Or, perhaps you found that you were in pretty good shape "weight"-wise. But *spiritual fitness* is a lot like *physical fitness.* You can fall within the guidelines of the height/weight/age chart, but lack the strength — the heart and muscle tone — to even lift a spoonful of cornflakes to your mouth!

• Based on the three passages in today's "diet," list three reasons it is important to be spiritually strong.

1._____

2._____

3._____

DAY 2

TODAY'S DIET: Read Psalm 96:7, Proverbs 24:10 & Daniel 11:32.
EXERCISE: Assess your spiritual strength.

1. When problems come, my *first* reaction is generally
   - ❑ to wonder why this has happened to me.
   - ❑ to wonder how I am ever going to get through it.
   - ❑ to pray.

2. As I deal with a problem,
   - ❑ I am easily frustrated and weary of it quickly.
   - ❑ I generally handle it well for a little while.
   - ❑ I generally handle it well for a relatively long period of time.

3. I know the Bible says "the people who know their God shall be strong, and carry out great exploits [bold deeds],"
   - ❑ but I have never carried out anything I would consider an "exploit" for God.
   - ❑ but I seldom carry out anything I would consider an "exploit" for God.
   - ❑ and I routinely carry out "exploits" for God.

DAY 3

TODAY'S DIET: Revelation 3:7-13; Psalm 29:11; 46:1
EXERCISE: No matter how much or how little spiritual strength we have, we can always use more. And the best way to build up spiritual muscles, according to 1 Timothy 4:7, is *exercise!*

Spiritual Muscle Builder #1: Be sure you're saved.
Have you trusted Christ as your personal Saviour? If not, that is the first step. God promises to give *His* people strength. If you have never trusted Christ as your Saviour, you are not one of God's children and cannot ever expect to be spiritually strong.

Accepting Christ is easy:

1. **Recognize that you are a sinner.** You cannot realize your need of salvation until you know that you are a sinner. (Isa. 53:6; Rom. 3:10; 5:12; 6:23)

2. **Confess your sins and ask forgiveness.** You are a free moral agent with the privilege of choice — to ask for or to reject His pardon. Therefore, to receive His grace, you must confess your guilt and plead for His mercy to cleanse you from all your sin. Your sin was already paid for, in full, by Christ's death on the cross and His resurrection from the tomb. You, however, must come to Him! (1 John 1:9; Rom. 10:9-10; Luke 13:3; 1 Pet. 1:18-19)

3. **Believe.** Our Lord imparts the benefits of Calvary — eternal life, joy, peace, happiness—to only those who believe. To believe on, or to believe in the Lord Jesus Christ is to believe or trust Him as your personal Saviour. You not only believe, appropriate, and accept the fact that He died for you and paid for your sins, but you receive Him personally into your life. You accept facts and receive a Person. (John 3:36; 5:24; Acts 16:31; Matt. 1:21; Isa. 1:18; Acts 4:12; John 1:12; Heb. 11:6; 1 John 5:11-12; John 3:16)

DAY 4

TODAY'S DIET: Read Acts 16:16-25.

EXERCISE: Notice that in both Acts 16:16 and 25, Paul and Silas were praying — the first time in their natural routine, the second time in jail after having been beaten! A spiritually strong person has a healthy, uninterrupted prayer life; and that prayer life, in turn, reciprocates, making the person even stronger! Notice also that in verse 25, Paul and Silas were singing; the joy of the Lord was overflowing their hearts despite their circumstances, and that joy was spilling out through their mouths in praise to God.

Spiritual Muscle Builder #2: Tone up your prayer life.
Assess and align your prayer life in the light of Psalm 105:4 and Isaiah 40:31.

Spiritual Muscle Builder #3: Focus on the positive.
Note the benefits of looking on the bright side of things (Neh. 8:10 and Ps. 118:14) and begin to make it a part of your routine lifestyle.

DAY 5

TODAY'S DIET: Acts 9:1-22

EXERCISE: After Saul's conversion, he spent time with the disciples in Damascus, no doubt discussing the Scriptures. Afterward, he immediately began working — preaching — and as a result he "increased all the more in strength."

Spiritual Muscle Builder #4: Read and Obey God's Word.
Assess and align your Scripture reading and memorization in the light of Deuteronomy 11:8 and Proverbs 24:5.

Spiritual Muscle Builder #5: Work.
Get involved in local church ministry. Do you have a personal ministry . . . a job you are routinely responsible for that you perform in or through a local church?

If not, begin to pray this week about the work God would have you to do.

PART 3
THE WEIGHT OF FRUSTRATION

7

BUT YOU DON'T KNOW MY HISTORY!

Though I walk in the midst of trouble,
You will revive me . . .
and Your right hand will save me.
The Lord will perfect that which concerns me.
— Psalm 138:7-8

As we began this study, we looked at some unique vessels — the vessels that were used in the service of the Lord in the tabernacle and in the temple. We discovered some unusual characteristics about those vessels:

1. They were prepared and offered for that service by prescribed weight.

2). They were designed for a lifetime of service; so they were formed from the valuable, durable, strong materials of the day, gold and silver.

We have also established in the previous chapters that since there is no more tabernacle and since there is no more temple, when we trust Christ as our Saviour, *we* become the vessels that God uses in His service. As vessels, *we* are set apart for a lifetime of service.

> For the gifts and the calling of God are irrevocable (Rom. 11:29).

> Being confident of this very thing, that He who has begun a good work in you will complete it until the day of Jesus Christ (Phil. 1:6).

And although we were created as vessels of clay, as believers, we receive the treasure of God's indwelling Spirit, making us valuable, and enabling us to be durable and strong.

Our theme verse, Hebrews 12:1 says, "Let us lay aside every weight, and . . . let us run with endurance the race that is set before us."

This race, this lifetime of service, is not a 50-yard dash. It's a marathon. Lap after lap. Mile after mile; and we can't afford to be carrying any extra weight — any burdens, cares, concerns, or debilitating habits.

After surveying hundreds of people, asking each to name the top three "weights" they felt were facing Christians in America today, one of the top 10 — in fact, one of the top 5 — was the weight of frustration.

Webster's Encyclopedic Dictionary defines frustration as being prevented from achieving an objective. It's having an attempt foiled. It's the feeling of being thwarted or baffled, feeling deprived of something you were due, or feeling like you have some fundamental need that is unsatisfied.

But probably the shortest and most explanatory definition is found in the Latin root word from which we get our word, *frustration.* That Latin root word simply means, *disappointment.* Disappointment is directly related to our expectations. When things don't go as we expect, we are frustrated.

Frustration in itself is not a sin, just as anger, in itself, is not a sin. The Bible says, "Be angry, and do not sin" (Eph. 4:26). But there is the *possibility* of sinning whenever anger is present; and the same is true with frustration. Frustration lives right next door to sin.

Did you ever notice how easy it is to gain that second pound after you've gained the first? Well, the same is true of excess spiritual poundage. Unless you learn to deal with — to "lay aside" — the initial weight of frustration, you risk picking up additional "pounds" before you know it.

Extra pounds like doubt . . . fear . . . anxiety . . . depression . . . stress-related disorders . . . maybe even a broken relationship or a habit that becomes a crutch.

And sadly, some who begin with an initial instance of frustration when life does not go as expected even wind up experiencing the final, fatal weight of suicide.

Return for a moment in your thinking to those temple vessels — those valuable, durable vessels, created and presented by weight, designed for a lifetime of service in Jerusalem.

For several hundred years those vessels fulfilled their purpose, service in the temple in Jerusalem; that is, until a powerful, conquering king, Nebuchadnezzar of Babylon, stormed through Jerusalem, destroying the city, burning the temple, taking captives, and, according to Jeremiah 52:19, taking back to Babylon those same temple vessels.

For a time the vessels disappear from biblical history; until they re-appear in the sacred record in Daniel 5.

The years have passed. Nebuchadnezzar's grandson, Belshazzar, has assumed the throne. Daniel records that Belshazzar had thrown a huge party for a thousand of his lords. During the evening, Belshazzar called for the confiscated temple vessels to be brought and used in the drunken festival praising the pagan gods of Babylon.

That very night, God stripped Belshazzar of his kingdom, gave it to Darius the Mede, who in turn was conquered by Cyrus the Persian.

Throughout these decades of Middle East turmoil, the temple vessels remained far from home; far from fulfilling the purpose for which they were created.

But once again the vessels surface on the pages of holy history — this time in the Book of Ezra the priest, in the form of a royal edict from Cyrus, king of Persia:

> Let the gold and silver articles of the house of God, which Nebuchadnezzar took from the temple which is in Jerusalem and brought to Babylon, be restored and taken back to the temple which is in Jerusalem, each to its place; and deposit them in the house of God (Ezra 6:5).

Ezra 1:7-10 continues the saga:

> King Cyrus . . . brought out the articles of the house of the Lord . . . and counted them out to . . . the prince of Judah.

The prince of Judah then turned the vessels over to Ezra the priest. And in Ezra 8:24-25 we read that Ezra called "twelve of the leaders of the priests . . . and weighed out to them . . . the articles."

Ezra told the priests,

> Watch and keep them [the temple vessels] until you weigh them before the leaders of the priests and the Levites and heads of the fathers' houses of Israel in Jerusalem, in the chambers of the house of the Lord. So the priests and the Levites received the silver and the gold and the articles by weight . . . departed . . . came to Jerusalem . . . and . . . on the fourth day the . . . articles were weighed in the house of . . . God . . . and all the weight was written down at that time (Ezra 8:29-34).

Notice that when the vessels returned home to the

temple they were *still gold* and *still silver* and once again they were weighed.

Their *value*, their *durability* and *en-durability* — their *strength* — as well as their *purpose* of a lifetime of service had not changed *even though both their location and the expectations concerning them had.*

Not one spoon had lost an ounce; and not one platter had gained a pound.

But how about you?

You the vessel.

You, the one God has called to a lifetime of service. You, the one upon whom God has placed great value. You, the one God has asked to be durable and strong.

When frustration takes you captive, do you maintain your luster?

How about your durability . . . your spiritual weight? Does it fluctuate with frustration?

Have you ever felt your faith slipping away ounce by ounce, being replaced by what seems like pounds and pounds of doubt or anger or fear?

If so, don't quit reading now. Hope and help are just a page or two away!

Let us lay aside the weight of frustration . . .
and let us run with endurance the race
that is set before us.
— based on Hebrews 12:1

8

ONE SIZE DOES
NOT FIT ALL

But Job said to his wife,
"You speak as one of the foolish women speaks.
Shall we indeed accept good from God,
and shall we not accept adversity?"
In all this Job did not sin with his lips.
— Job 2:10

Frustration comes in all sizes. There are major frustrations, such as when a devastating illness strikes, or
when you're laid off the job after 20 years with the
same company. But frustration also comes in medium, small,
and minuscule sizes like when you lock your keys in the
car . . . or get eggshell in the cookie dough.

Frustration can come in the form of spilled milk and
shattered glass all over the kitchen floor . . . . a button that
pops off when you're already late for work . . . a phone
that's busy, or that keeps you on hold for an eternity, or that
rings while you're in the shower or sound asleep in the
middle of the night.

Frustration can result from sitting in your car behind someone trying to turn left at the busiest intersection, or from sitting in your doctor's office 45 minutes

past your appointment time.

There is no question that frustrations come. But the question is, how are you dealing with them? And how are we *expected* to deal with them?

In the "exercises" in the earlier chapters of this book, you were asked to first assess your spiritual weight and then your spiritual strength, or your durability and your endurability. But if you were to go for a *physical* fitness assessment, the fitness specialist would not only check your weight and strength and endurance, but also your *flexibility*.

> Flexibility is the ability to move a joint fluidly through its complete range of motion. . . . Flexibility can be improved greatly by including stretching exercises in the daily routine.[1]

> The major limitation to both static and dynamic flexibility is the tightness of soft tissue structures.[2]

So let's take a moment and begin to assess your *spiritual* flexibility.

> • How well do *you* move through a day's complete range of motion?
> • Are you so uptight that your spiritual flexibility is limited?
> • Is it possible that God is allowing some of the frustrations in your daily routine in order to stretch you spiritually?

Spiritual flexibility is a requirement if you're going to successfully run with endurance — and win — the race that God has set before you.

We find both flexible and *in*flexible people in Scripture. Take Jonah, for instance. God told Jonah, "Go to Nineveh." Jonah refused (Jon. 1:1-3). He was inflexible — stiff-necked.

Paul wanted to go to Bithynia. But God said, "No, go

to Macedonia." So Paul went (Acts 16:7-10). When his travel plans were frustrated, he was flexible.

SO . . .

• What makes the difference between someone who's flexible (able to handle frustration — unfulfilled expectations) and someone who's not?

• If you are inflexible, how do you become more flexible?

• And if you're carrying the weight of frustration, how do you "lay it aside" as Hebrews 12:1 encourages?

Spiritually flexible people *know* four things and *do* three things.

FOUR THINGS SPIRITUALLY FLEXIBLE PEOPLE KNOW

1. Everyone has frustration.

> He [your Father in heaven] makes His sun rise on the evil and on the good, and sends rain on the just and on the unjust (Matt. 5:45).

> These things I have spoken to you, that in Me you may have peace. In the world you will have tribulation (John 16:33).

> No temptation has overtaken you except such as is common to man (1 Cor. 10:13).

2. All frustration is either planned or permitted by God.

We call this the sovereignty of God. He can and does do as He pleases.

He always has had, and always will have, absolute control over everything and everyone in the entire universe. No creature, person, empire, force, or law of nature can act contrary to His will in any way.

All frustrations are subject to Him. Frustrations cannot touch a child of God unless God himself permits it.

Even our mistakes and failures, as well as the mistakes and failures of others that frustrate us — even the willful, malicious acts of others — are subject to His sovereign will.

Jerry Bridges in his book, *Trusting God,* makes this statement:

> Nothing is so small or trivial as to escape the attention of God's sovereign control; nothing is so great as to be beyond His power to control it. The insignificant sparrow cannot fall to the ground without His will; the mighty Roman empire cannot crucify Jesus Christ unless that power is given to it by God (Matt. 10:29; John 19:10-11). And what is true for the sparrow and for Jesus is true for you and me. No detail of your life is too insignificant for your heavenly Father's attention; no circumstance is so big that He cannot control it.[3]

When that car door slammed shut, locking your keys inside, God was not surprised.

He permitted the eggshell to fall in the cookie dough.

The loss of your job . . . the death of your spouse . . . the discovery of your cancer did not occur outside of His sovereign will, His infinite wisdom or His perfect love.

> Who is he who speaks and it comes to pass, when the Lord has not commanded it? Is it not from the mouth of the Most High that woe and well-being proceed? (Lam. 3:37-38).

> I form the light and create darkness, I make peace and create calamity; I, the Lord, do all these things (Isa. 45:7).

> There are many plans in a man's heart, Nevertheless the Lord's counsel — that will stand (Prov. 19:21).

> In whom also we have obtained an inheritance, being predestined according to the purpose

of Him who works all things according to the counsel of His will (Eph. 1:11).

There is no wisdom or understanding or counsel against the Lord (Prov. 21:30).

I know that You can do everything, and that no purpose of Yours can be withheld from You (Job 42:2).

For the Lord of hosts has purposed, and who will annul it? His hand is stretched out, and who will turn it back? (Isa. 14:27).

Indeed before the day was, I am He; and there is no one who can deliver out of My hand; I work, and who will reverse it? (Isa. 43:13).

The third thing spiritual flexible people know is this:
3. Frustrations come from various sources and for a variety of reasons.

• Some frustrations are natural consequences. If you only allow the exact amount of time needed to get to the office under optimal conditions, and instead of optimal conditions, you hit every red light, your frustration is a natural consequence.

• Some frustrations are the results of the laws of nature. If your child bumps the full glass of milk on the table hard enough, the law of gravity takes over and you have a mess.

• Some frustrations are the result of our own foolishness, poor planning or poor organization, or failure to align our plans with God's.

Someone said we spend half our lives looking for things. That's a frustration caused by poor organizational skills.

We complain about the airlines over-booking flights, and yet we're probably all guilty of over-booking our time, over-estimating our ability and over-extending ourselves.

Why wouldn't we get frustrated?!

• Some frustrations are the result of our sinful nature — our pride . . . ingratitude . . . selfishness.

When you're behind that guy trying to turn left at the busiest intersection in the world, it's easy to think, "*I* would *never* do anything that stupid or inconsiderate." But the truth is, we all do things just as ill-advised . . . things that frustrate others just as much as that guy ahead is frustrating you.

And when, upon occasion, we do acknowledge that we have made a mistake, it's suddenly very easy to remember that *we* are *dust*; but when it comes to the other guy, all to often, he's just plain *mud!*

And talk about ingratitude. So what if you have to sit 45 minutes past your appointment time in the doctor's waiting room? Why be frustrated? Why not focus on how fortunate you really are?

You're waiting for the most advanced health care in the history of the world. Your chances for comfort and survival are greater than ever before. A few years ago you could have waited *days* for a doctor to arrive in a horse and buggy to tell you there was nothing he could do!

And the next time that guy wants to turn left in front of you, remember: you don't have to be in a car behind him . . . you could be walking.

• Some frustrations are to test us.

Satan accused Job of serving God just because God had blessed him. God allowed Satan to take away everything — Job's wealth, his health, even his children — and still Job served God.

> Though He slay me, yet will I trust Him (Job 13:1).

Jesus told Peter (Luke 22:31) that Satan had asked to be able to test Peter — to sift him as wheat. Peter failed the initial test, denying the Lord three times. Yet it was Peter who wrote this encouragement concerning frustration:

In this you greatly rejoice, though now for a little while, if need be, you have been grieved by various trials, that the genuineness of your faith, being much more precious than gold that perishes, though it is tested by fire, may be found to praise, honor, and glory at the revelation of Jesus Christ (1 Pet. 1:6-7).

• Some frustrations are to force us to change directions as when Paul tried to go to Bithynia.
• Some frustrations are chastisement like Jonah's encounter with the whale.

Do not despise the chastening of the Lord, nor be discouraged when you are rebuked by Him; for whom the Lord loves He chastens . . . for our profit, that we may be partakers of His holiness. Now no chastening seems to be joyful for the present, but grievous; nevertheless, afterward it yields the peaceable fruit of righteousness to those who have been trained by it (Heb. 12:5-11).

• Many are God-sent opportunities in disguise.
Joseph's brothers sold him into slavery. While in Egypt, Joseph faced multiple frustrations including imprisonment on false charges. His response when his brothers finally were forced to face up to their evil deed? A classic!

Joseph said to them, "Do not be afraid, for am I in the place of God? But as for you, you meant evil against me; but God meant it for good, in order to bring it about as it is this day, to save many people alive" (Gen. 50:20).

The last thing spiritually flexible people know is that:
4. *All* frustration can be significantly reduced or prevented all together — laid aside — so we can run and *win* the race.

But we have this treasure in earthen vessels,

that the excellence of the power may be of God and not of us. We are hard pressed on every side, yet not crushed; we are perplexed, but not in despair; persecuted, but not forsaken; struck down, but not destroyed. . . . Therefore we do not lose heart. Even though our outward man is perishing, yet the inward man is being renewed day by day. For our light affliction, which is but for a moment, is working for us a far more exceeding and eternal weight of glory" (2 Cor. 4:7-17).

The key is spiritual flexibility. Knowing these four things. And doing the three things described in the following chapter.

Let us lay aside the weight of frustration . . . and let us run with endurance the race that is set before us.
— based on Hebrews 12:1

Endnotes

[1] Vivian H. Heyward, *Designs for Fitness, a Guide to Physical Fitness Appraisal and Exercise Prescription* (Minneapolis, MN: Burgess Publishing Company, 1984), p. 4.

[2] *Ibid., p. 140.*

[3] Jerry Bridges, *Trusting God* (Colorado Springs, CO: NavPress, 1988).

9

WHIPLASH

Furthermore the Lord spoke to me, saying,
"I have seen this people,
and indeed they are a stiff-necked people."
— Deuteronomy 9:13

If your car has ever been rear-ended, you probably wound up with a bit of a stiff neck, if not full-blown whiplash. Frustration also has a way of riding your emotional bumper and slamming into you from behind when you least expect it. Frustration can also cause a bit of a stiff neck — something that can be easily worked out of the spiritually flexible person's system.

But if we're not careful, that "bit of a stiff neck" can intensify to the point where we feel whipped — physically exhausted, emotionally drained, spiritually defeated.

The key to avoiding "whiplash" is spiritual flexibility. God says,

> Now do not be stiffnecked, as your fathers were, but yield yourselves to the Lord; and enter His sanctuary, which He has sanctified forever, and serve the Lord your God (2 Chron. 30:8).

And Psalm 78:1 says,

> Give ear, O My people, to My law; Incline
> your ears. [Tip your head, rotate that neck, be flex-
> ible!] Incline your ears to the words of My mouth.

Spiritually flexible people *do* three things. These three
things are actually neck exercises and they're easy to remember and do: Look up. Look in. Look out!

1. LOOK UP.

• When frustration comes, acknowledge God's role in
it. Consciously tell yourself, "God has allowed this to happen to me at this time. *God* allowed me to lose my job . . . to
lock my keys in my car . . . to be behind this person trying
to turn left. This could not have happened outside of God's
sovereign will, His infinite wisdom or His perfect love.

• Seek wisdom and insight.

If any of you lacks wisdom, let him ask of God, who
gives to all liberally and without reproach [without making
you feel stupid for asking], and it ill be given to him (James
1:5).

Ask questions.
Why did God allow this frustration?
What is its real source? (Review previous chapter.)
What, God, do you want me to learn from it?
Is there an opportunity here?
Is it time for me to change directions?
Is this a test? Or could it be chastisement?

• Ask for help.

> Let us therefore come boldly to the throne
> of grace, that we may obtain mercy and find grace
> to help in time of need (Heb. 4:16).

2. LOOK IN

Really look. How flexible is your heart? Will it open up enough to think of the self-esteem of the child who spilled the milk? Or is it too uptight to think of anything but having to clean up the shattered glass on the floor?

Is it so hardened with pride and self-righteousness that you can't forgive the mistakes — maybe even the sheer stupidity — or the crass selfishness of the guy trying to turn left at the busiest intersection in the world?

Can you see people as God sees *all* of us?

The same people who provided the greatest frustration to Christ and His message were the very ones He had compassion on. People like impetuous Peter who sank beneath the waves. People like Mary and Martha who blamed Jesus for not coming earlier when Lazarus was just sick and not dead. The disciples who argued about who would be greatest in the kingdom of God. The nine lepers He healed who never even bothered to say thank you. People like me. Like you . . .

> And be kind to one another, tenderhearted, forgiving one another, just as God in Christ also forgave you (Eph. 4:32).

Is your heart pliable enough to be humble . . . even to repent if that's what's called for to lay aside a particular frustration?

Will it bend enough to make necessary changes in foolish over-extension . . . to allow enough time for getting to the office even when *all* the lights are red?

Will it be inclined to improve poor planning . . . to improve bad organization skills?

Exercise that stiff neck. Don't suffer whiplash. Look Up. Look In. Then . . .

3. LOOK OUT!

• Look out for others.

Let nothing be done through selfish ambition or conceit, but in lowliness of mind let each esteem others better than himself. Let each of you look out not only for his own interests, but also for the interests of others. Let this mind be in you which was also in Christ Jesus (Phil. 2:3-5).

Love one another fervently with a pure heart (1 Pet. 1:22).

But I say to you, love your enemies, bless those who curse you, do good to those who hate you, and pray for those who spitefully use you and persecute you (Matt. 5:44).

Now we exhort you, brethren, warn those who are unruly, comfort the fainthearted, uphold the weak, be patient with all. See that no one renders evil for evil to anyone, but always pursue what is good both for yourselves and for all (1 Thess. 5:14-15).

• Look out for your own testimony.

You are the salt of the earth; but if the salt loses its flavor, how shall it be seasoned? It is then good for nothing but to be thrown out and trampled under foot by men (Matt. 5:13).

• Look out for opportunities.

Remember when Paul expected to go to Bithynia and God redirected him to Macedonia? That's the beginning of the story.

The rest of the story is the story of the Philippian jailer: Paul and Silas singing at midnight in the jail . . . God sending an earthquake and opening the doors . . . the jailer ready to kill himself . . . and that famous verse in Acts 16:31:

Believe on the Lord Jesus Christ and thou shalt be saved.

What was an initial frustration became an important opportunity.

But remember those temple vessels that were carried off into Babylon? Well, they weren't alone. People — God's people . . . Jews . . . thousands of them — were also carried off into Babylon. In fact, some of our favorite Bible stories date back to that time and from that place — stories of Daniel, Shadrach, Meshach, Abednego, Ezekiel, Jeremiah, Ezra, Nehemiah, Esther.

That initial frustration — Jews carried off into the Babylonian captivity — became an important opportunity for a man by the name of Daniel to rise to leadership and testify before the very captor himself — King Nebuchadnezzar.

If that frustration — that *opportunity* — had not come, King Nebuchadnezzar might never have praised Jehovah God as he did (Dan. 4:34-37).

And what about those three Hebrew children in the fiery furnace? (Dan. 3). What kind of a testimony do you think they had? And how far do you think it reached?

And what about Daniel in the lion's den? What a testimony he was to King Darius the Mede! (By the way, did you know that the Medes are the ancient ancestors of the modern-day Kurds?)

It was in the land of frustration in the time of captivity that some said,

> By the rivers of Babylon, there we sat down, yea, we wept, when we remembered Zion. We hung our harps upon the willows in the midst of it. . . . How shall we sing the Lord's song in a strange land? (Ps. 137:1-4).

But it was also there, in the land of frustration in the time of captivity, that Daniel faced Zion and prayed confidently three times a day.

It was also there, in the land of frustration in the time

of captivity, that he received the vision of the end times, recorded in Daniel 2, one of the greatest foundational prophetic passages in all of Scripture.

What was the difference between the harp-hangers and Daniel?

Spiritual flexibility.

Daniel had learned the secret of daily neck exercise. He had learned to *look up* and acknowledge God's sovereignty, wisdom and love. Daniel had also learned to *look in.* He was willing to confess his own inadequacy and to identify with a nation who had forgotten God (Dan. 9:2-19).

And Daniel was willing to *look out* for his people by claiming the promise of God to end the captivity . . . to look out for his testimony even if it meant death in the lions' den . . . and to avail himself of every frustration-cloaked opportunity that God sent his way.

Daniel had the ability to incline his heart toward God . . . to lay aside the frustration of being a captive in a foreign land in order to run a race that God had set before him.

Now it's your turn.

———————————

Let us lay aside the weight of frustration . . .
and let us run with endurance the
race that is set before us.
— based on **Hebrews 12:1**

PART 3
LET US LAY ASIDE THE WEIGHT OF FRUSTRATION

In a recent survey, hundreds of people were asked to name the top three "weights" they felt were facing Christians in America today. One of the "Top Ten" was *frustration*.

Webster's Encyclopedic Dictionary defines frustration as: being prevented from achieving an objective; having an attempt foiled; the feeling of being thwarted or baffled, feeling deprived of something you were due, or feeling like you have some fundamental need that is unsatisfied.

But probably the shortest and most complete definition, and the one easiest for us to identify with, is found in the Latin root word from which we get our word, *frustration*. That Latin root word simply means *disappointment*. Disappointment is directly related to our expectations. When things don't go as we expect, we can pick up the heavy weight we have come to call *frustration*.

DAY 1

TODAY'S DIET: Jon. 1:1-3; 3:1-5; 4:1-11

EXERCISE: Frustration in itself is not a sin . . . just as anger, in itself, is not a sin. The Bible says, "Be angry, and do not sin" (Eph. 4:26). But the *possibility* of sinning is there. Just as it is easier, physically speaking, to pick up that *second* pound after you have gained the *first, it is easy to pick up more spiritual weight if the initial weight of frustration is not effectively dealt with.*

• After reading today's Scripture diet, consider the following list of additional weights.

Which did Jonah pick up after his initial frustration?

Are there any *you* have a tendency to pick up when *you* are frustrated?

What can you learn from Jonah that will help you deal with your frustration?

_____
_____
_____
_____

DAY 2

TODAY'S DIET: Acts 15:40; 16:7-12, 22-33
EXERCISE: In Parts 1 and 2 of this series, you assessed your spiritual weight and then your spiritual strength and endurance. But if you were to go for a *physical* fitness assessment, your *flexibility* would also be evaluated.

> Flexibility is the ability to move a joint fluidly through its complete range of motion. . . . Flexibility can be improved greatly by including stretching exercises in the daily routine.
>
> The major limitation to both static and dynamic flexibility is the tightness of soft tissue structures.[1]

• How *is* your *spiritual* flexibility?

• How well do *you* move through a day's complete range of motion?

• Are you so uptight that your *spiritual flexibility* is limited?

• Is it possible that God is allowing some of the frustrations in your daily routine in order to *stretch* you spiritually?

Spiritual flexibility is a requirement if you're going to successfully run with endurance and win the race God has set before you.

• After reading today's "diet," write down one thing that impressed you about the spiritual flexibility of the apostle Paul.

_____
_____
_____

DAY 3

TODAY'S DIET: Matthew 5:45; John 16:33; 1 Corinthians 10:13

EXERCISE: Spiritually flexible people know *that everyone has frustration*. Read Hebrews 4:14-16. This passage confirms that not only is frustration common to mankind, it was also experienced by the Son of Man, the Lord Jesus Christ.

• According to verse 14, we can be encouraged to face frustration successfully — without letting it lead to sin.

• According to verse 15, what is a major step toward accomplishing that feat?

_____
_____
_____

DAY 4

TODAY'S DIET: Isaiah 64:8; Jeremiah 18:1-4

EXERCISE: Spiritually flexible people also know *that all frustration is either planned or permitted by God.* Think about your home or car insurance policy. Chances are, it calls floods, tornadoes, and other natural disasters "acts of God." Based on today's "diet," do you agree with that terminology or not?

• Consider the way you think about the "providence of God." Is it easier for you to accept the good things in life as "providence," but hard for you to accept the frustrations of life as equally providential?

• If so, add these Scriptures to your daily diet until you feel more fortified in this area:

Lamentations 3:37-38	Isaiah 45:7
Proverbs 19:21	Ephesians 1:11-12
Psalm 115:3	Isaiah 14:27
Isaiah 43:13	

DAY 5

TODAY'S DIET: 2 Corinthians 4:7-17

EXERCISE: A third thing spiritually flexible people know is that *all frustration can be significantly reduced or prevented all together (laid aside, according to our theme verse) so we can run — and win — the race.*

• Scripture calls spiritually *inflexible* people *stiffnecked.* Second Chronicles 30:8 gives us this encouragement: "Now do not be stiffnecked . . . but yield yourselves to the Lord."

• The following "spiritual neck exercises" will help you become spiritually flexible when dealing with frustration:

1. **Look Up.**
   When frustration comes, acknowledge God's role in it. (Lam. 3:37-38; Isa. 14:27; 43:13; 45:7; Prov. 19:21; Eph. 1:11; Ps. 115:3)

   Ask for wisdom and insight concerning the source and reason for the frustration (James 1:5).

   Ask for help to successfully deal with the frustration (Heb. 4:16).

2. **Look In.**
   Psalm 137:1-2, 4 and the life of Jonah vs. the book and life of Daniel.

3. **Look Out!**
   For others (Phil. 2:3-5; 1 Pet. 1:22; Matt. 5:44; 1 Thess. 5:14-15).
   For your testimony (Matt. 5:13).
   For opportunities (Acts 16; the Books of Daniel, Ezra, Nehemiah, Esther).

Endnotes
[1]Vivian H. Heyward, *Designs for Fitness* (NEED CITY/STATE: PUBLISHER, YEAR), p. 4 and 140.

PART 4
THE WEIGHT OF GUILT

10

"PUNISH ME, PLEASE!"

*I fell on my knees and spread out my hands
to the Lord my God, and said,
"O my God: I am too ashamed and humiliated
to lift up my face to You, my God;
for our iniquities have risen higher than our heads,
and our guilt has grown up to the heavens."*
— Ezra 9:5,6

A few years ago, a child molester/murderer on death row faced the battle of his life as the hour approached when he would, by court order, receive a final, fatal injection.

A group of do-gooders, convinced that lethal injection constituted cruel and unusual punishment, was seeking a court order staying the man's execution.

The man, however, along with his attorney, also filed a brief with the court, asking it to *not* stay the execution. In addition, the man petitioned the governor to *not* pardon him. And the do-gooders were asked to kindly butt out.

The man *wanted* to die. He *wanted* to pay the penalty for his crime. He was tired of fighting the feelings of guilt as well as the urge to molest and murder again.

At about the same time, we surveyed hundreds of

people, asking them what they felt were the greatest hindrances Christians in America today are facing. One of the top answers was *guilt.*

The Merriam Webster Dictionary defines guilt as:

1. the fact of having committed an offense, or
2. a feeling of responsibility for offenses.

According to our survey, then, a large percentage of respondents felt that *Christians* in America today are not only *committing* offenses, but they are unable to rid themselves of the *feeling of responsibility* for those offenses.

And in addition, many people also carry a weight of guilt for incidents over which they had no control — victims of abuse, for instance . . . children of alcoholic or divorced parents . . . and a whole bunch of us who have made honest mistakes sometime in the past.

But innocent or not, shouldering a lifetime load of guilt is the exact opposite of the way it ought to be! Remember, God's Word says:

Let us lay aside every weight, and let us run
with endurance the race that is set before us (Heb.
12:1).

But when dealing with the subject of guilt, it's important to add verse 2 and verses 12-14 as well:

Looking unto Jesus, the author and finisher
of our faith, who for the joy that was set before
Him endured the cross.

Therefore strengthen the hands which hang
down, and the feeble knees, and make straight
paths for your feet, so that what is lame may not
be dislocated, but rather be healed.

Pursue peace . . . and holiness, without which
no one will see the Lord.

There are three things we must notice in addition to our theme verse:

1. First of all, the Cross is the remedy for both the *fact* and the *feeling* of guilt.

> But God demonstrates His own love toward us, in that while we were still sinners, Christ died for us (Rom. 5:8).

> And you . . . He has made alive . . . having forgiven all your trespasses, having wiped out the handwriting of requirements that was against us, which was contrary to us. And He has taken it out of the way, having nailed it to the cross (Col. 2:13-14).

> For the wages of sin is death, but the gift of God is eternal life in Christ Jesus our Lord (Rom. 6:23).

> And He Himself is the propitiation for our sins, and not for ours only but also for the whole world (1 John 2:2).

2. The second thing to notice in those verses is the pursuit of holiness. In other words, Christians are not to be found *routinely* guilty of committing offenses.

3. The final thing to note in those verses is the *pursuit of peace.* Christians are not be guilt-ridden. Rather, we are to consciously lay aside guilt and be peaceful.

Yet thousands of Christians today are ineffective and unhappy because we are weighted down with a load of guilt. Thousands of us are seeking comfort from pills and counselors. We return to altars time after time after time to cry and confess; but we leave nearly as comfortless as we came to await the next altar call. And all this, even though Jesus said,

> I am the way, the truth, and the life (John 14:6).

You shall know the truth, and the truth shall make you free (John 8:32).

Therefore if the Son makes you free, you shall be free indeed (John 8:36).

There is therefore now no condemnation to those who are in Christ Jesus, who do not walk according to the flesh, but according to the Spirit (Rom. 8:1).

Therefore, having been justified by faith, we have peace with God through our Lord Jesus Christ, through whom also we have access by faith into this grace in which we stand, and rejoice in hope of the glory of God (Rom. 5:1-2).

Maybe you know one of these people. Maybe you *are* one of these people.

Maybe today *you* are the one carrying a load of guilt. Maybe it's just a little. . . . Maybe it's a lot. Maybe it's because of something you said or did yesterday. Maybe it's something from the distant past. A bad choice you made . . . or maybe it was something in which you had no choice at all. At a wild party. Or in a sterile clinic . . . or a back alley. Maybe on Wall Street. Or in your home as a child . . . or as an adult in a church you used to attend.

Maybe today you want more than anything to be free from the guilt — to lay aside the weight — but you just don't know how.

Be assured. Based on God's eternal Word, you can know how. And once you learn and activate the scriptural principles for dealing with guilt, you're guaranteed to run the race a whole lot more easily and with a greater degree of endurance than you ever thought possible.

So go get the key to that closet from the past. Because the skeletons you've kept locked up in there are ready to rattle their way out of your life forever!

Let us lay aside the weight of guilt . . .
and let us run with endurance
the race that is set before us.
— based on Hebrews 12:1

11

KNOW YOUR GUILT

O Lord God of Israel . . .
here we are before You, in our guilt.
— Ezra 9:15

G uilt is one of the timeless companions of mankind. But fortunately, just as timeless are the mysterious divine principles of overcoming guilt.

These principles are what David the adulterer learned that enabled him to look unashamedly into the eyes of his son, Solomon. They are the precepts that empowered him to turn over the rule of God's people and the building of God's house to the son of Bathsheba, the woman whose husband he had murdered.

These principles enabled Peter to face the risen Lord whom he had denied three times with a vile oath.

They are the reason Paul could stand before the relatives of Christians he had ordered bound and killed. They are why he could confess to them that he was chiefest of sinners, then preach such a powerful and persuasive message that those same grieving relatives would believe, and embrace him as a brother in Christ.

These principles are why the woman taken in adultery could face her accusers and walk away guilt-free while *they* left one by one, ashamed, convicted by their own consciences.

But they're more than that. They're how *you* can know true freedom from guilt as well — no matter what you've said or done.

These principles are how *you* can face the wife whose heart you broke . . . or the child you only see on weekends. They're how *you* can pay without bitterness the monthly installments on something you know you never should have bought.

They're the reason you can go on and try again after you've picked up that pack of cigarettes . . . that glass of booze . . . that bottle of pills . . . that you promised you had set down for the last time.

They're how you can pray . . . and know you've been heard.

They're how you deal — not only with long-term guilt, but with the daily, short-term guilt trips . . . like when your son tells you the cookies you sent to the class party were the only ones that weren't homemade. Like when your husband asks you if you picked up his suit at the cleaners, and you haven't . . . like when your secretary asks if you returned that urgent call and you didn't.

You see, guilt is a universal human experience.

But the principles for dealing with guilt are also universal because they were designed by the Creator of the universe. And He recorded them for us in His Word.

Furthermore, He promised that what worked for David and Peter and Paul will work for you. It works on little guilt trips as well as on full-blown guilt cruises.

But it only works when you identify the kind of baggage you're lugging along on the trip. In other words . . .

KNOW YOUR GUILT

There are two kinds of guilt, and you need to learn to distinguish between them. There is *ob*jective guilt and there is *sub*jective guilt

*Ob*jective guilt is true moral guilt. It's a fact. It's when you break a law — the law of man or a law of God — knowingly or unknowingly.

When you don't stop at a red light, you are objectively guilty, whether you saw the light or not, because there is a law on the books that says everyone must stop at all red lights. If you rob or kill or covet or hate, you *are* guilty whether you *feel* guilty or not.

> Now we know that whatever the law says, it says to those who are under the law, that every mouth may be stopped, and all the world may become guilty before God. Therefore by the deeds of the law no flesh will be justified in His sight, for by the law is the knowledge of sin. . . . For all have sinned and fall short of the glory of God (Rom. 3:19-23).

That's *ob*jective guilt.

But there is also *sub*jective guilt. *Sub*jective guilt is the *feeling* of guilt.

The interesting thing is, you can feel guilty even when you're not. You can also feel guilty when you are — when your conscience has been violated.

Not everyone, however, feels guilty about the same things. But everyone does feel some form of guilt at some time — a sense of failure or shame — when their own particular conscience is violated — when a personal standard has been broken.

Even professional hit men have a conscience based on their own personal code of ethics. For instance, they'll kill a mark on the street in a heartbeat; but they won't drop even the biggest contract in a church — because then they'd feel guilty!

Many rapists have no qualms about raping . . . robbers about robbing . . . drug dealers about selling. But they do have a conscience of sorts. Most for instance, are intolerant of child molesters. That's why child sex offenders are often kept in solitary confinement — to keep the other bad guys from killing them — for conscience sake!

You see, in its purest form, *sub*jective guilt — or the *feelings* of guilt — are God's way of working through mankind's conscience to get us to recognize sin and do something about it.

God himself did the initial programming of the human conscience. It's innate . . . inborn. That's why even a toddler hesitates — if only for a second — when Mommy says, "No."

But in addition to this basic programming, God also provided man with a general knowledge of himself . . . of truth . . . and of right, or righteous, behavior:

> For the wrath of God is revealed from heaven against all ungodliness and unrighteousness of men, who suppress the truth in unrighteousness, because what may be known of God is manifest in them, for God has shown it to them. For since the creation of the world His invisible attributes are clearly seen, being understood by the things that are made, even His eternal power and Godhead, so that they are without excuse (Rom. 1:18-20).

Furthermore, God imprinted moral law in the human heart — or in the conscience, of man:

> For when Gentiles, who do not have the law, by nature do the things contained in the law, these, although not having the law, are a law to themselves, who show the work of the law written in their hearts, their conscience also bearing witness, and between themselves their thoughts accusing or else excusing them (Rom. 2:14-15).

All of these — the inborn conscience . . . the general revelation of God, truth and righteousness . . . the moral law

. . . were designed by a loving Heavenly Father in order that He might maintain some form of touch-point with fallen man.

He established a basis for man to feel guilty — not so His children would be tormented days without end — but so a sinful race could still be reached . . . and redeemed. And that's where God's Holy Spirit comes in — to nudge the conscience:

> Nevertheless I [Jesus] tell you the truth. It is to your advantage that I go away; for if I do not go away, the Helper will not come to you; but if I depart, I will send Him to you. And when He has come, He will convict the world of sin, and of righteousness, and of judgment: of sin, because they do not believe in Me; of righteousness, because I go to My Father and you see Me no more; of judgment, because the ruler of this world is judged (John 16:7-11).

Feeling guilty when we are guilty — *sub*jective guilt — is a tool of God's love and mercy. It's God's way of needling us to mend a tear in our relationship with Him and with others. It's that feeling of being pricked in the heart — and it's designed to send us running to the cross:

> Now when they heard this [that they had crucified Jesus, the Savior], they were cut to the heart, and said to Peter and the rest of the apostles, "Men and brethren, what shall we do?" Then Peter said to them, "Repent, and let every one of you be baptized in the name of Jesus Christ for the remission of sins" (Acts 2:37-38).

The problem is that many of us have not learned how to leave guilt — all of it — both kinds of it — at the cross. We find forgiveness for sin and truly believe that we will never have to answer for it or pay for it again. That takes care of *ob*jective guilt.

But we leave the cross still carrying a heavy load of *sub*jective guilt. We still *feel* guilty . . . we still feel ashamed . . . like a failure. We are just as disappointed in ourselves as we were before we climbed the hill to Calvary.

If this sounds like someone you know or someone you are, read on. Because Calvary really does cover it all.

Let us lay aside the weight of guilt . . .
and let us run with endurance
the race that is set before us.
— based on Hebrews 12:1

12

DEAL WITH IT!

You have turned for me my mourning into dancing;
You have put off my sackcloth
and clothed me with gladness. . . .
O Lord my God, I will give thanks to You forever.
— Psalm 30:11-12

Many of us are weight-lifters extraordinaire when it comes to guilt. We've pumped it and pressed it . . . lifted and lugged it. But unlike other kinds of weights that trim us and tone us, the weight of guilt leaves us physically drained, emotionally limp, and spiritually flabby. And not surprisingly so, because guilt — particularly leftover, unwarranted feelings of guilt — are a slap in the face of Almighty God.

In the last section, we discovered that there are two kinds of guilt:

1. actual or *ob*jective guilt when a law has been broken, and

2. *sub*jective guilt — the feelings of guilt.

We also learned that the first step to losing the heavy weight of guilt is identifying which kind of guilt you are experiencing. It may be one or both. But whichever it is, the next step is to deal with it.

DEALING WITH OBJECTIVE GUILT

(when you're really guilty of doing something wrong)

Objective guilt is actual guilt. It means you have done something wrong. You have broken a law. You have sinned.

Objective guilt — sin — requires the payment of a penalty. A personal penalty. God says that penalty is death:

> The wages of sin is death (Rom. 6:23).

> The soul who sins shall die. The son shall not bear the guilt of the father, nor the father bear the guilt of the son. The righteousness of the righteous shall be upon himself, and the wickedness of the wicked shall be upon himself (Ezek. 18:20).

But while sin with its objective guilt demands payment of a death penalty, God provided that payment for anyone willing to accept and receive it:

> For the wages of sin is death, *but the gift of God is eternal life in Christ Jesus our Lord* (Rom. 6:23).

> But God demonstrates His own love toward us, in that while we were still sinners, Christ died for us. Much more then, having now been justified by His blood, we shall be saved from wrath through Him (Rom. 5:8-9).

> For God so loved the world that He gave His only begotten Son, that whoever believes in Him should not perish but have everlasting life (John 3:16).

The required death penalty for sin was paid in full by Christ at Calvary. And anyone can be rid of the weight of sin — actual, objective guilt — by confessing and forsaking it at the Cross.

He who covers his sins will not prosper, *but whoever confesses and forsakes them will have mercy* (Prov. 28:13).

If we confess our sins, He is faithful and just to forgive us our sins and to cleanse us from all unrighteousness (1 John 1:9).

That if you confess with your mouth the Lord Jesus and believe in your heart that God has raised Him from the dead, you will be saved. For with the heart one believes to righteousness, and with the mouth confession is made to salvation (Rom. 10:9-10).

But in a sense, that's the easy part. Getting rid of the actual guilt. Forsaking sin and being forgiven. *Feeling* forgiven, however, is often quite another matter.

DEALING WITH SUBJECTIVE GUILT

(when you feel guilty . . . whether you are or not)

Unlike objective guilt, *sub*jective guilt has no penalty and requires no payment; yet this is one of the areas that Satan uses most to defeat us. It's where the real *weight* of guilt comes in. The guilt that God never intended us to bear. The weight that is assumed by far too many Christians.

It can slip into our lives so subtly . . . even after we've confessed our sin. After God has forgiven us. And sometimes when we weren't guilty of anything in the first place!

As we've already studied, God gives each person a conscience, intended as a useful tool of the Holy Spirit. Those initial feelings of guilt when we are, in fact, guilty — the ones that lead us to recognize and confess our sin — are a gift from God.

But like so many gifts from God, Satan craftily attempts to substitute a counterfeit conscience — unjustified feelings of guilt that linger after God has forgiven and forgotten the sin. Or, in some cases, when there was no sin to begin with. These unjustified feelings of guilt rob us of our joy, can make our lives ineffective and unproductive, and our testimony impotent.

Not only does Satan attempt to keep us from confessing our sin in the first place, he also rejoices and helps us *feel* guilty even after we *have* confessed our sin. He whispers — and in effect, often convinces us — that Christ's death was not enough . . . that God did not mean what He said, and that we must, ourselves, do something more to be free.

When this kind of a weight of guilt attempts to take over our lives, we need to fling the Scriptures in Satan's face as Christ did in His time of temptation (Matt. 4). There are many wonderful verses suitable for face-flinging. (They're also pretty comforting for us!) Some favorites are:

> Therefore, having been justified by faith, we have peace with God through our Lord Jesus Christ, through whom also we have access by faith into this grace in which we stand, and rejoice in hope of the glory of God (Rom. 5:1-2).

> The sting of death is sin, and the strength of sin is the law. But thanks be to God, who gives us the victory through our Lord Jesus Christ (1 Cor. 15:56-57).

> There is therefore now no condemnation to those who are in Christ Jesus (Rom. 8:1).

You see, subjective guilt — *feelings* of guilt after sin has been confessed — rejects Christ's work at Calvary. When you feel guilty after God has forgiven you (or when you were never guilty of anything to begin with) it is the result of the devil's lie. And it's a dangerous trick of the enemy that pushes you precariously near the brink of blasphemy.

So what's the bottom line? How do you get rid of the ugly weight called guilt? The Scriptures teach four basic principles:

1. Learn to distinguish between and deal with the two kinds of guilt.

If your cookies were the only ones that weren't home-made, decide if by not baking cookies, you violated a moral law. Was it sin or not? If it was, confess it. And even if it wasn't, talk it through with your child. And in either case, let go of the feelings of guilt.

Make that a common practice anytime you feel guilty: distinguish and deal with it. Are you guilty or are you just *feeling* guilty?

Pray as the psalmist prayed:

> Search me, O God, and know my heart; Try me, and know my anxieties; And see if there is any wicked way in me, And lead me in the way everlasting (Ps. 139:23-24).

2. Then, get on with your life.

Claim God's forgiveness and power. Focus on the promises God has made concerning freedom from sin and guilt:

> I [God] will forgive their iniquity, and their sin I will remember no more (Jer. 31:34).

> As far as the east is from the west, So far has He removed our transgressions from us (Ps. 103:12).

> You [God] will cast all our sins into the depths of the sea (Mic. 7:19).

God doesn't dwell on your past or the bad feelings connected with it; so why should you?

> Not that I have already attained, or am already perfected; but I press on, that I may lay

hold of that for which Christ Jesus has also laid hold of me. Brethren, I do not count myself to have apprehended; but one thing I do, forgetting those things which are behind and reaching forward to those things which are ahead, I press toward the goal for the prize of the upward call of God in Christ Jesus (Phil. 3:12-14).

Finally, brethren, whatever things are true, whatever things are noble, whatever things are just, whatever things are pure, whatever things are lovely, whatever things are of good report, if there is any virtue and if there is anything praiseworthy — meditate on these things (Phil. 4:8).

3. Discipline yourself to respond to the promptings of the Holy Spirit, and to reject the whispering of the devil.

Anytime you begin to feel the least bit guilty, discipline yourself to practice discernment. Distinguish and deal with it!

And do not be conformed to this world, but be transformed by the renewing of your mind, that you may prove what is that good and acceptable and perfect will of God (Rom. 12:2).

4. Get involved in a local church.

Have you ever noticed how popular going to the gym is becoming? Or how many body toning videos are available? Why is that?

It's because we are social creatures. God made us that way. After creating Adam, He said, "It's not good for man to be alone." And He created Eve.

And the fact is that we lose more pounds and tone more flab when we're not doing it alone. Even if the other person is Richard Simmons on tape!

The same is true when it comes to setting aside spiritual weights — like guilt, for instance. You see, God never intended for you to lose it and keep it off all by yourself. He has provided help — not just at the cross . . . not just through prayer . . . not just through His Word . . . but through His church — people who want to help lift the weight . . . who have experience in distinguishing true and false guilt, people with expertise to help you understand God's forgiveness . . . and who will provide personal encouragement.

God said,

> Confess your trespasses to one another, and pray for one another, that you may be healed. The effective, fervent prayer of a righteous man avails much (James 5:16).

The forum for that setting is the local church. And your place is in church — either to be helped by others . . . or to help others . . . or better yet, both.

Let us lay aside the weight of guilt . . .
and let us run with endurance
the race that is set before us.
— based on Hebrews 12:1

PART 4
LET US LAY ASIDE THE WEIGHT OF GUILT

In a recent survey, hundreds of people were asked to name the top three "weights" they felt were facing Christians in America today. One of the "Top Five" was *guilt.*

The Merriam Webster Dictionary defines guilt as (1) the *fact* of having *committed an offense,* or (2) a *feeling of responsibility* for offenses.

According to the survey, then, a large percentage of respondents felt that Christians in America today are not only *committing* offenses, but they are unable to rid themselves of the feelings of responsibility for those offenses. And that's the exact opposite of the way it ought to be!

DAY 1

TODAY'S DIET: Hebrews 12:1-2,12-14; Romans 6
EXERCISE: While Hebrews 12:1 encourages us to lay aside the weight of guilt, verses 2 and 12-14 outline three basic principles that must be accepted before the weight of guilt can be lost:

> 1. The cross is the remedy for both the *fact* and the *feeling* of guilt.
> 2. Christians are to "pursue holiness" *(verses 13,14).* They are not to be *routinely guilty* of committing offenses.
> 3. Christians are to "pursue peace" *(verses 14)* rather than being guilt-ridden. They are to consciously lay aside guilt and be peaceful.

• Do you know someone who is constantly troubled with feelings of guilt?

If so, write that person's name here and begin to earnestly pray for them this week: _____

Ask the Lord to open a door for you to share the scriptural

truths about guilt with them.

• Are *you* sometimes overwhelmed with a feeling of guilt? If so, begin to earnestly pray this week that the Lord will imprint the scriptural truths about guilt upon *your* heart to help you lay aside this extra weight you are carrying.

DAY 2

TODAY'S DIET: Psalm 38
EXERCISE: The weight of guilt has far-reaching effects. David wrote in Psalm 38:4 that his iniquities had gone over his head; they were "like a heavy burden . . . too heavy" for him.

• As you read Psalm 38, note the verses that describe how David's guilt affected him:

> spiritually – verse
> physically – verse
> emotionally – verse
> psychologically – verse
> socially – verse

• Which of the above effects have you seen Christians experiencing as a result of guilt?

• Have you personally ever experienced any of the above effects as a result of feeling guilty?

• In the last verses of this psalm, David cries out, "Do not forsake me, O Lord; O my God, be not far from me! Make haste to help me, O Lord, my salvation!"

Make that your prayer today. Ask the Lord to reveal to you if any of the effects you are currently experiencing — physically (headaches, etc.), emotionally, in a relationship, and so on — are related to underlying guilt.

DAY 3

TODAY'S DIET: Romans 3:19-23
EXERCISE: To lay aside the weight of guilt, it is impor-

tant to first distinguish between the two kinds of guilt: *obj*ective guilt and *sub*jective guilt.

• Objective guilt is true moral guilt. It's a fact. There was a law — of man or God — and you broke it, knowingly or unknowingly. You are the *object* of a broken law.

• Objective guilt demands payment of a penalty, but that penalty was paid in full at Calvary for everyone who chooses to accept it as such, according to John 3:16, Romans 3:23, 5:8-9 and 6:23.

• Everyone is born guilty — including you. The only way to get rid of that guilt is to trust Christ as your personal Saviour. If you have never done that, study today's verses and Romans 10:9-10.

• Whenever we sin — even after salvation — that sin automatically carries with it objective guilt. But we can be cleansed from that guilt by confession since the penalty for it, too, was paid at Calvary.

• Commit these two verses to memory this week if you have not already:

> He who covers his sins will not prosper, but whoever confesses and forsakes them will have mercy (Prov. 28:13).

> If we confess our sins, He is faithful and just to forgive us our sins and to cleanse us from all unrighteousness (1 John 1:9).

DAY 4

TODAY'S DIET: Romans 1:18-21; 2:14-15; John 16:7-11
EXERCISE: *Sub*jective guilt is the *feeling* of guilt. It occurs when the conscience is violated. Everyone has a conscience, and guilt is a universal human experience.

• God himself does the initial programming of the conscience.

He has placed within each person a general knowledge of himself, of truth, and of righteousness through creation (Rom. 1:18-21).

He has imprinted the moral law in the heart — the conscience — of man (Rom. 2:14-15).

God sent His Holy Spirit to reprove, convince and convict the world (John 16:7-11).

• In its purest form, subjective guilt is a tool of God's love and mercy. It's God's way of needling us to mend a tear in our relationship with Him and with others.

• Subjective guilt has no penalty and requires only that we accept the payment that was already made at Calvary. Once we have confessed sin, and accepted the price paid at Calvary for that sin, the feelings of guilt will be laid aside.

• Are you currently grappling with guilt? If so, read Psalm 139:23-24. Make it your prayer.If God reveals sin for which you ought to feel guilty, confess it.

DAY 5

TODAY'S DIET: Psalm 119:15-16; Philippians 4:4-8; Romans 12:1-2

EXERCISE: Too many times after we confess our sin, we still feel guilty. What God intended as a useful tool of the Holy Spirit — the conscience, or the feelings of guilt — Satan counterfeits, robbing us of our joy, making our lives ineffective and unproductive, and our testimony impotent.

• Not only does Satan attempt to keep us from confessing our sin in the first place, he also rejoices and helps us *feel* guilty even after we have confessed our sin.

• He whispers — and seemingly convinces us — (1) that Christ's death was not enough, and (2) that God did not mean what He says when He says we are forgiven and that our sin is forgotten, and (3) that we must, ourselves, do something more to be free.

• Do you ever feel guilty even after you have confessed sin in your life?

Rehearse the following verses internally, and maybe even out loud the next time Satan — or anyone else — tries to make you feel guilty for something you have already settled with God:

1 JOHN 1:7-9

7 But if we walk in the light as He is in the light, we have fellowship with one another, and the blood of Jesus Christ His Son cleanses us from all sin.

8 If we say that we have no sin, we deceive ourselves, and the truth is not in us.

9 If we confess our sins, He is faithful and just to forgive us our sins and to cleanse us from all unrighteousness.

ROMANS 5:1-2

Therefore, having been justified by faith, we have peace with God through our Lord Jesus Christ, through whom also we have access by faith into this grace in which we stand, and rejoice in hope of the glory of God.

ROMANS 8:1-6

1 There is therefore now no condemnation to those who are in Christ Jesus, who do not walk according to the flesh, but according to the Spirit.

2 For the law of the Spirit of life in Christ Jesus has made me free from the law of sin and death.

3 For what the law could not do in that it was weak through the flesh, God did by sending

His own Son in the likeness of sinful flesh, on account of sin: He condemned sin in the flesh,

4 That the righteous requirement of the law might be fulfilled in us who do not walk according to the flesh but according to the Spirit.

5 For those who live according to the flesh set their minds on the things of the flesh, but those who live according to the Spirit, the things of the Spirit.

6 For to be carnally minded is death, but to be spiritually minded is life and peace.

1 CORINTHIANS 15:56-57

The sting of death is sin, and the strength of sin is the law. But thanks be to God, who gives us the victory through our Lord Jesus Christ.

JEREMIAH 31:34

For I will forgive their iniquity, and their sin I will remember no more.

PSALM 103:12

As far as the east is from the west, So far has He removed our transgressions from us.

MICAH 7:19

He will again have compassion on us, and will subdue our iniquities. You will cast all our sins into the depths of the sea.

13

DREAM ON!

You have sown much, and bring in little;
you eat, but do not have enough;
you drink, but you are not filled with drink;
you clothe yourselves, but no one is warm;
and he who earns wages,
earns wages to put into a bag with holes.
Thus says the Lord of hosts: "Consider your ways!"
— Haggai 1:6-7

I t was June 1885. Packing cases — 214 of them, containing 225 tons of material — arrived in New York Harbor. Day after day, the crates were unpacked, and a proud lady rose on a pedestal overlooking Ellis Island.

She was, of course, the Statue of Liberty — a monumental tribute to the hundreds of thousands of immigrants who flocked to America in the 1800s alone. Unemployed immigrants who proudly took jobs in the factories, creating America's industrial revolution . . . starving immigrants from Ireland . . . persecuted immigrants from Holland . . . 9,000 Chinese who labored to lay the rails of the great Union Pacific across our land . . . farmers from Sweden and Norway who claimed and tamed the midwestern prairies.

It was the fulfillment of the American Dream in all its

glory — challenge . . . adventure. An education for every child. Jobs with pay. Food on the table. The opportunity to own your own land and home. Freedom to worship.

But now, for many, the American Dream has degenerated into a nightmare of financial pressure.

Many of us — the great-great-grandchildren of those immigrants — now look at the uncertainty ahead and are overwhelmed. Our youth face a future where, with even a low annual inflation rate, a two-dollar Big Mac will skyrocket to $13 within their lifetime. A movie ticket to $47. A $17,000 car to nearly $125,000. And a $100,000 home to three-quarters of a million dollars!

Is it any wonder that teenage suicides have become the second leading cause of death for young people — topped only by car accidents? These young people, full of energy and life, should be seeing, seeking — and finding — the American Dream; but instead, they're cashing it all in before they've even given it a try.

Adults are also feeling the ever-increasing weight of economics. Major companies are downsizing, creating massive layoffs of loyal, hardworking, long-term employees. Those of us lucky enough to retain our jobs wind up working nearly three hours every day just to pay federal, state, and local taxes. Meanwhile, the costs of child care, child-rearing and college tuition have soared.

It's no wonder then, that financial pressure is now a major contributing factor in 90 percent of all divorce cases . . . which are also escalating beyond previously known heights.

But that's not the way the American Dream is supposed to work. The Dream is supposed to guide any willing, hard-working American gently and steadily toward financial independence and comfortable retirement.

Yet for many of us, the closer we get to our golden years, the more elusive the pot at the end of the rainbow becomes. Dollars saved years before are now worth pennies. Social Security checks threaten to bounce; and many of us who have built our lives believing in the American Dream . . . who have practiced and preached it . . . may live to see that dream debilitate and die.

Why has this happened in America of all places — the Land of Opportunity? Why are so many of us afraid that the financial weight we now carry will crush the American Dream?

The answer may lie in a 1990 survey conducted by Mark Clements Associates. Notice its findings:

> While 80 percent of those . . . questioned say they spurn money as the ultimate symbol of success, they also concede that they feel controlled by it. Again, 80 percent say that, in some real ways, money limits how they live, where they work and how their children are brought up.

In other words, instead of us controlling our money, money is controlling us — and it's determining our decisions, our dispositions — and our destiny. It's become a weight that God never intended for us to bear.

The fact is, during Jesus' earthly ministry, He mentioned money — getting it . . . spending it . . . saving it — more than any other single topic He taught about. Interested in what He had to say? Then turn the page and prepare to receive some of the most personal and personalized financial counseling available anywhere!

Let us lay aside the weight of financial pressure . . .
and let us run with endurance
the race that is set before us.
— based on Hebrews 12:1

14

A GOLDEN DOOR, OR WINDOWS OF HEAVEN

And all the tithe of the land . . . is the Lord's.
— Leviticus 27:30

So you shall rejoice in every good thing which the Lord
your God has given to you and your house. . . .
When you have finished laying aside all the tithe [10
percent] of your increase then you shall say before the
Lord your God: "I have removed the holy tithe from my
house." — Deuteronomy 26:11-13

"Bring all the tithes into the storehouse...
and prove Me now in this," says the Lord of hosts,
"If I will not open for you the windows of heaven
And pour out for you such blessing
That there will not be room enough to receive it.
— Malachi 3:10

Her real name is "Liberty Enlightening the World," and for many years now, the Statue of Liberty has symbolized the American Dream.

Her golden torch lit the way for many from joblessness and starvation in foreign countries to a paycheck and regular meals; the shackle at her feet symbolized the personal financial freedom life in America guaranteed for so many years.

On her pedestal, a sonnet entitled "The New Colossus" by Emma Lazarus appears. It reads, in part,

> A mighty woman with a torch, whose flame
> is the imprisoned lightning, and her name Mother
> of Exiles. . . . . "Give me your tired, your poor,
> Your huddled masses yearning to breathe free.
> Send these, the homeless, tempest-tost [sic] to me,
> I lift my lamp beside the golden door!"

But for many of us today, that golden door of financial freedom has slammed shut. Our fiscal world is far from enlightened, and the "Newest Colossus" in our lives is the most recent stack of unpaid bills. In short, the American Dream has become a nightmare of financial pressure.

The Bible says that as God's people are faithful in their giving to God, He will pour out blessings . . . prosperity . . . financial success. Yet many Christians today — even faithful tithers — have not had the windows of heaven opened, but are instead struggling with money matters as much as those who have never given God a dime.

Perhaps this describes you. Perhaps you have lost the American Dream. Perhaps you have little hope of owning your own home . . . of putting your children through college . . . of ever retiring comfortably.

That's financial pressure. And it's a weight God never intended for you to bear. Now that doesn't mean that there won't be times when you'll have financial reverses, because God tests us in just about every area of our lives at one time or another.

But over the long haul, God wants us to "lay aside every weight" that is pulling us down and slowing us down — and that includes the weight of financial pressure.

But how do we do that? What is the problem? Why

are the windows of heaven shuttered to so many of us? Obviously the problem is not with God . . . or His Word. More than likely, the problem lies in our relying upon — and practicing — the financial principles found in His Word.

Paul said to the church at Rome, "Faith comes by hearing, and hearing comes by the Word of God" (Rom. 10:17).

Faith *comes*. It wasn't there, or it wouldn't need to come. And it comes when we hear the Word of God — when we *really* hear it — and activate the principles in our life. Then, and only then, do we really learn how to "lay aside the weights that so easily beset us."

So what does God say about our the future — and our finances? In Jeremiah 29:11, He says,

> I know the thoughts that I think toward you,
> says the Lord, thoughts of peace, and not of evil,
> to give you a future and a hope.

In 2 Timothy 1:7 we read,

> For God has not given us a spirit of fear; but
> of power and of love and of a sound mind.

The "us" is that verse refers to Christians — believers. God has not given a spirit of fear to Christian believers — those who believe that Jesus died for their sin and rose again.

Now, if you're not a believer, you have every reason to be afraid. Because you don't have a Heavenly Father looking out for you; and you ought to be afraid of the havoc that's coming on this earth — financial havoc, included.

But for the Christian, God has not given us a spirit of fear; He's given us a spirit of power . . . a spirit of love and a sound mind.

That phrase "sound mind" is literally a combination of two Greek words, the first meaning "safe," and the second meaning "mind." It denotes perception — the ability to see and make the right decisions. It involves good judgment, disciplined thinking, and self-control.

In other words, a sound mind does not panic. It does not allow the matter of finances to become pressure or weight. A sound mind operates on the solid principles of Scripture. A sound mind makes and saves and spends and invests money based on those principles, and therefore controls financial matters without pressure — "weightlessly."

The Bible teaches tithing — giving 10 percent of your income — to God; but it also teaches many more strategies for successfully handling money and prospering. If you are a faithful tither, but failing to practice those other principles, you are missing a major portion of God's financial plan. And you may be keeping the windows of heaven shut up tight.

It would be like trying to believe in the Cross but not the Resurrection as it pertains to your salvation. The Bible says:

> For to this end Christ died and rose and lived again (Rom. 14:9).

And when Paul wrote Timothy, he made it very clear. He said we are saved "if we believe that Jesus died and rose again" (1 Thess. 4:14).

You can't separate the death of Jesus on the cross from His resurrection. We must, if we're going to be saved, believe simultaneously in His death on the cross and His resurrection.

So it is with the matter of finance. We must understand the whole counsel of God. There's more than one principle; and there's more to fiscal freedom that just bringing God His tithe and our offerings.

Fortunately, the other principles work (as does tithing) for anyone of any age — because they are God's principles. And they work whether you have a lot or money or whether you have no money — because they are eternal principles.

Paul said to young Timothy,

> Let no one despise your youth, but be an example to the believers in word, in conduct, in love, in spirit, in faith, in purity (1 Tim. 4:12).

David, as a senior citizen, said,

> I have been young, and now am old; yet I have not seen the righteous forsaken, nor his descendants begging bread (Ps. 37:25).

And Jesus said,

> But seek first the kingdom of God and His righteousness; and all these things shall be added to you (Matt. 6:33).

You see, the ability to make, save, spend, and use money wisely is a God-given privilege. The question is — and always has been — Are you ready to assume responsibility for that privilege?

Let us lay aside the weight of financial pressure . . .
and let us run with endurance
the race that is set before us.
— based on Hebrews 12:1

15

IT'S THE PRINCIPLE OF THE THING

Delight yourself also in the Lord,
And He shall give you the desires of your heart.
— Psalm 37:4

Even the best of us can use an occasional sprucing up. Lady Liberty's took four years and $66 million. That's three times longer and four times the number of original francs she cost.

That's the way it is with fixing things up. It's often expensive and time-consuming. That's why we should begin a financial weight loss program as soon as the first ounce of fiscal pressure appears. And it's why we should all stay on a financial weight *maintenance* program — forever. Because fixing it costs time and money none of us has to spare.

God's financial weight loss/maintenance program has three main principles. Number 1 is basic.

PRINCIPLE #1: GET A GOOD EDUCATION . . . THE BEST JOB YOU CAN . . . AND THEN WORK AT IT!

The immigrants who built modern America sought education for their children, came for the jobs America offered, and worked hard after they got here. That's part of the American dream. It's also part of God's financial plan.

> For a dream comes through much activity (Eccles. 5:3).

Let's look briefly at each of the three aspects of Principle #1. First of all, *Get a good education.* Getting a good education involves more than getting a GED or graduating from high school or college. Getting a good education is a life-long process. It means you are constantly learning.

The person who *doesn't* read is no better off than the person who *cannot* read. Both are limited. America is rich with learning resources; and if you want to prosper financially, you need to take advantage of them.

Turn off the television and read a book. Or change your video diet and check out the educational and discovery channels. Enroll in night school. Take advantage of free or inexpensive seminars. Listen to inspirational or educational cassettes in your car. Surf the Net with purpose. Or — do something drastic and visit a library again. You see, there's really no excuse to be ignorant, out-of-touch, out-of-date, or uninformed in America.

"But," you might say, "what about Jesus' disciples? They were unlettered. They hadn't gone to school."

Anyone who says that has forgotten that these men the critics called "unlearned and ignorant" (Acts 4:13), spent three years, 24 hours a day, with Jesus, the Master Teacher. They actually finished their doctorates in theology, medicine, psychology, demonology, and a whole bunch of other-ologies in record time!

God is a strong supporter of higher education:

> Study to show thyself approved unto God, a workman that needeth not to be ashamed (2 Tim. 2:15;KJV).

Fools despise wisdom and instruction (Prov. 1:7).

Fools hate knowledge (Prov. 1:22).

Wise people store up knowledge (Prov. 10:14).

Through wisdom a house is built, and by understanding it is established; by knowledge the rooms are filled with all precious and pleasant riches (Prov. 24:3).

Obviously the Bible links education and knowledge with prosperity. But even the 1990 United States census concurs. According to its data, men ages 35 to 44 with four years of college were earning 60 percent more than men of the same age with only a high school education. Over an average career, that means the college graduate will take home nearly a half-million dollars more than the high school graduate.

So if you're a young person, get a good education. And no matter what age you are, keep learning! Plus — *Get the best job you can . . . and then work at it.* God rewards the laborer and allows the lazy to suffer the natural consequences of lethargy:

He who gathers by labor will increase (Prov. 13:11).

The sluggard [lazy] will beg during harvest and have nothing (Prov. 20:4).

The desire of the slothful [lazy] kills him, for his hands refuse to labor (Prov. 21:25).

Be not lagging in diligence, fervent in spirit, serving the Lord (Rom. 12:11).

If anyone will not work, neither shall he eat (2 Thess. 3:10).

Have you ever had someone wave a sign at you that says, "Will work for food?" Have you ever noticed that generally within a few blocks there's another sign — on a local business — that says, "Help wanted?"

There are many jobs available for people who really want to work. The pay may not be great, the hours may be tough, and the work may not be particularly fun. But God promises to bless — to increase — the laborer. And God's benefits far outweigh poor pay, lousy hours, and even the worst of work.

God says focus on being and doing, not on having. Yet the primary concern of the average job applicant is not, "What can I be?" or "What can I do?" but "What do I get?"

Being and doing was the secret of Joseph's rise to power in Egypt. You remember that when he was 17 years old, Joseph was sold to be a slave in a foreign land by his own brothers. Joseph could have wallowed in self-pity, but instead he focused on what he could be and what he could do. He rose from the ranks of common slavery to being the household manager for a prominent military leader, and from there to being the prime minister of Egypt — second in command to Pharaoh himself.

Joseph prospered because of his personal commitment, discipline, and plain old hard work in whatever position he found himself. He prospered because he following a scriptural principle.

PRINCIPLE #2: FOLLOW A FORMULA

It's amazing to think that even if you earn only $20,000 a year, in 20 years you will make $400,000 . . . in 30 years, $600,000 . . . in 40 years, $800,000! If you make $30,000 a year, in 40 years you will make $1.2 million.

That's a lot of money.

So how you *feel* about money — your *attitude* — and how you *handle* money — your *actions* — are important, not only to you, but to God.

There are probably as many financial formulas around as there are financial consultants, but one formula that has worked for many is the 10-10-10-70 Formula:

The first 10 percent of income to God;
the second 10 percent to debt;
the third 10 percent to savings;
the remaining 70 percent to live on.

It works like this. You honor God by giving Him *the first 10 percent* of your income. The whole 100 percent is really His, anyway.

The earth is the Lord's, and all its fullness,
The world and those who dwell therein (Ps. 24:1).

And you shall remember the Lord your God, for it is He who gives you power to get wealth (Deut. 8:18).

It's not that God needs your 10 percent; it's that He wants us to acknowledge His ownership of the 100 percent. He is the owner, we are the administrators. And when we honor Him with the first 10 percent, He has promised to honor and prosper us.

Honor the Lord with your possessions, and with the firstfruits of all your increase; So your barns will be filled with plenty (Prov. 3:9-10).

Take it off the top. Give God the first dollar out of every ten. Give Him the first hour of every day. Give Him the first consideration in every decision. Put Him first, and then, He says "Your barns will be filled with plenty."

The second 10 percent goes to debt. There is no long-term debt carried longer than seven years in the Bible. And being debt-free is a scriptural principle.

Owe no man any thing, but to love one another (Rom. 13:8).

Ten- and twenty- and thirty-year loans are a modern "convenience." And gratefully so, since it is always better to own a house than it is to rent. Especially when it is possible — if you buy a home that is commensurate with your financial base — to reduce a long-term loan from 30 years to 15, or from 15 to 7.5 by following scriptural principles.

Take *the third 10 percent* and use it as capital for investment. Make it work for you, earning interest or dividends . . . or buying equity . . . somehow broadening your financial base. Investment is a biblical principle.

> The plans of the diligent lead surely to plenty (Prov. 21:5).

Study Matthew 25:14–29. It's the story of a man who distributed talents (pieces of money, each worth about $1,000) to his servants. He gave one servant five talents; another, two talents; a third servant, one talent.

The first servants invested their talents and doubled their money. The third servant hid his.

When the man returned to settle the accounts and received the same amount back from the third servant as he had given him originally, he was angry, and said:

> You ought to have deposited my money with the bankers, and at my coming I would have received back my own with interest. Therefore take the talent from him, and give it to him who has ten talents. For to everyone who has, more will be given, and he will have abundance: but from him who does not have, even what he has shall be taken away (Matt. 25:27–29).

A savings account may not double your money, but it will at least increase it with interest. The point is, don't spend everything you have. Give 10 percent to God, apply 10 percent to debt, and invest 10 percent to broaden your financial base.

Finally, live on 70 percent . . . and beware of borrowing. The Bible says, "The rich rules over the poor, And the borrower is servant to the lender" (Prov. 22:7).

Borrowing is a doorway to bondage. And that pocketful of credit cards is heavier than you think — it may even be a financial weight that's dragging you down and slowing you down more than you ever dreamed possible.

The American Dream has been replaced largely by a literal credit craze. In 1994 the outstanding consumer credit debt of America was nearly $985 billion — almost 20 percent of our disposable personal income — approximately $4,000 for every one of the 248 million of us.

In just 50 years — from 1940 to 1990 — credit card debt increased one hundred-fold. No doubt there are many Christians — even tithing Christians — caught up in this tremendous web of debt . . . despite what God said about borrowing.

If you can't afford to buy something now with 70 percent of your income, think long and hard about borrowing to buy it. And think even longer and harder before borrowing to buy something that depreciates as soon as your purchase it — unless you are already debt-free.

If something you buy is not worth more when you sell it than what you paid for it, it is unwise to buy it with borrowed money.

PRINCIPLE #3: CHANGE YOUR LEVEL OF FINANCIAL THINKING

Einstein said, "The significant problems we face cannot be solved at the same level of thinking we were at when we created them."

Financial problems cannot be solved on the same superficial level on which they were created.

It doesn't require a great deal of thinking or a very deep level of thinking to spend or borrow or use a credit card. It's easy. Because the devil and the world system that he controls is a financial snare set to snap — and trap you

— in financial bondage.

> Do not love the world or the things in the world. If anyone loves the world, the love of the Father is not in him. For all that is in the world — the lust of the flesh, the lust of the eyes, and the pride of life — is not of the Father, but is of the world. And the world is passing away, and the lust of it; but he who does the will of God abides forever (1 John 2:15–17).

> And do not be conformed to this world, but be transformed by the renewing of your mind, that you may prove what is that good and acceptable and perfect will of God (Rom. 12:2).

> If any of you lack wisdom, let him ask of God (James 1:5).

Put God first. Study financial trends. Think before you spend. Pay off debt as quickly as possible. Watch for sound investments. And put Matthew 6:33 into practice:

> But seek first the kingdom of God and His righteousness, and all these things shall be added to you.

You see, it's not that God doesn't want you to have "things." It's that He doesn't want "things" to become your priority. Because "things" cost, and cost often leads to financial bondage — weight that will slow you down in your walk with Him and your race to win.

Let us lay aside the weight of financial pressure . . .
and let us run with endurance
the race that is set before us.
— based on Hebrews 12:1

PART 5
LET US LAY ASIDE THE WEIGHT
OF FINANCIAL PRESSURE

In a recent survey, hundreds of people were asked to name the top three "weights" they felt were facing Christians in America today. One of the "Top Ten" was *financial pressure.*

DAY 1

TODAY'S DIET: Luke 12:13-34

EXERCISE: For many years, the American dream has become a reality for thousands of people from many lands, offering challenge and adventure, an education for every child, jobs with pay, enough food to keep from starving, the opportunity to own your own home, and the freedom to worship.

• What does the American dream mean to you personally?

_____

_____

_____

_____

• For many of us today, the American dream has become a nightmare of financial pressure — so much so, that it has become a major contributing factor in nearly 90 percent of all divorce cases.

• A 1990 survey found that while 80 percent of those questioned rejected money as the ultimate symbol of success, all 80 percent also felt controlled by it, and all 80 percent said that money limits how they live, where they work, and how their children are brought up.

• Prayerfully *and honestly* consider the following questions as you begin to assess whether or not *you* are under a weight of financial pressure:

How do *you* measure the success of another?
Of yourself?
Do you measure it in terms of material assets alone?
List other factors you consider.

_____

_____

_____

To what degree do *you* feel controlled by money?
Do you feel that money limits how *you* live? Where
    you work?
Do you feel money limits how you are bringing up
    your children?

• Consider the following chart illustrating costs of the future. The figures given are based on an annual inflation rate of only 3.1 percent.

ITEM	price in 1997	price in 2057
Big Mac	$ 2	$ 13
movie ticket	$ 7	$ 47
golf clubs	$ 550	$ 4,000
car	$ 17,000	$125,000
home	$103,000	$750,000

• When you consider rising costs and your financial future, are you more hopeful or more fearful?

• Memorize Jeremiah 29:11 this week. Use it as a personal anchor and be ready to share it with others who are struggling with uncertainty concerning their financial future:

    For I know the thoughts that I think toward
    you, says the Lord, thoughts of peace, and not of
    evil, to give you a future and a hope.

• Read Psalm 37:25. It is important to keep in mind that God's blessings are promised specifically to believers who are walking with Him. If you have never trusted Christ as your personal Saviour, or if you are a believer living in disobedience, God may use financial pressure to cause you to seek Him out.

DAY 2

TODAY'S DIET: Matthew 6:19-21
EXERCISE: When considering financial matters, 2 Timothy 1:7 is a good verse to keep in mind: "For God has not given us a spirit of fear; but of power and of love and of a sound mind."

In the original Greek, the words *sound mind* are the equivalent of *safe-thinking,* denoting good judgment, disciplined thought patterns, and the ability to understand and make right decisions. It involves *self-control* and *self-discipline,* important principles when it comes to the matter of money.

• The first step in God's plan for losing financial weight is to get a good education, get the best job you can, and then work at it.

Read the following verses. Mark **E** if the verse applies to education, **W** if it applies to work, or **B** for both:

___Proverbs 13:11	___2 Timothy 2:15
___Proverbs 20:4	___Proverbs 21:25
___Proverbs 1:7	___Romans 12:11
___Proverbs 1:22	___2 Thessalonians 3:10

DAY 3

TODAY'S DIET: Matthew 6:33; Malachi 3:8-11; Psalm 50:10-12; Proverbs 3:9-10
EXERCISE: Consider the following chart. The potential for you handling a lot of money in your lifetime is very high. So how you *feel* about money — your *attitude* — and how you *handle* money — your *actions* — are important — not only to you, but to God.

EARNINGS TO RETIREMENT

straight projection (total earnings until retirement, assuming no increase in salary for promotions and no inflationary adjustments)

Annual	Years to Retirement				
Salary	40	30	25	20	15
$60,000	2,400,000	1,800,000	1,500,000	1,200,000	900,000
$50,000	1,000,000	1,500,000	1,250,000	1,000,000	750,000
$40,000	1,600,000	1,200,000	1,000,000	800,000	600,000
$30,000	1,200,000	900,000	750,000	600,000	450,000
$20,000	800,000	600,000	500,000	400,000	300,000

• Following a formula that is based on scriptural principles will help you keep financial matters from every becoming a weight; instead, they'll become bearable — and maybe even fun!

THE 10-10-10-70 FORMULA

- • Give the first 10 percent of your income as tithe.
- • Use the second 10 percent of your income to reduce debt.
- • Use the third 10 percent as capital for investment.
- • Learn to live on the remaining 70 percent.

• **The first 10 percent — tithe:** God instituted the tithe for *our* benefit, not *His* — to remind us that He owns it all — the whole 100 percent of our income. Giving 10 percent back to God is a systematic reminder for us that it's all His . . . but that He allows us to manage it for Him. It's also a test of our love and obedience to God.

Are you currently tithing? If not, why not?

• Some say that believers today are not required to tithe because the tithe was instituted under the Mosaic Law. If you have thought that, consider the following:

Abraham paid tithes *before* the law (Heb. 7:5-9).
Jesus said the tithe *ought* to be paid (Matt. 23:23).
Paul encouraged systematic giving based on income
   (1 Cor. 16:1-2).

• Read today's Scripture diet if you have not already. What blessings does God promise to those who honor Him with the first 10 percent of their income?

_____

_____

_____

• How would these blessings change the life of anyone carrying the weight of financial pressure?

• If you are not already tithing, begin. If you are, continue. And in either case, claim and look for the blessings God has promised.

• Read Matthew 25:22-23. How does being responsible with a small thing like 10 percent of our income affect the possibility of greater responsibility in the kingdom of God?

DAY 4

TODAY'S DIET: Romans 13:8; Proverbs 22:7; 1 John 2:15-17

EXERCISE: For many, the American Dream has been replaced by a credit craze . . . even though it is a scriptural principle that we be debt-free.

• The second 10 percent — debt reduction: On a separate sheet of paper, itemize your debt. If you cannot commit 10 percent of your next paycheck to debt reduction, decide how much you can apply.

• Take a responsible look at the number of credit cards you carry and the balances due on each. If you have used them unwisely and fallen prey to the hazards mentioned in the 1 John passage of today's "Scripture diet" — confess your weakness to God, and immediately lay aside as many of these small plastic "weights" as you can.

DAY 5

TODAY'S DIET: Proverbs 21:5; Matthew 25:14-29

EXERCISE: The third 10 percent — capital for investment: Which of the three servants in Matthew 25 are you most like? Why?

• **The remaining 70 percent — money to live on:** Are you spending more than 70 percent each month to live on? If so, why?

> Einstein said, "The significant problems we face cannot be solved at the same level of thinking we were at when we created them."

• If finances have become a weight, you must change your level of thinking. Financial problems cannot be solved on the same superficial, natural level on which they were created. Memorize Romans 12:2: "And do not be conformed to this world, but be transformed by the renewing of your mind, that you may prove what is that good and acceptable and perfect will of God."

• Learn how to live on 70 percent of your income. Spend wisely. Shop rather than buy. *Take as much time to spend as you do to earn.*

> **Tell yourself:** "The money I am about to spend took ___ hours of *my life* to earn."

> **Ask yourself:** "Is this something I *need,* or something I *want?* Is there a cheaper model or a store brand that would serve me just as well?"

> **Search yourself:** "*Why* do I want this? Is there any element of pride involved?" If so, read James 4:6 and Proverbs 16:18.

• If you are uncertain about financial decisions, seek godly counsel (Prov. 11:4) and ask for God's help (James 1:5).

> But seek first the kingdom of God and His righteousness; and all these things shall be added to you (Matt. 6:33).

16

JUST ONE OF THE GANG

My son, hear the instruction of your father,
and do not forsake the law of your mother. . . .
If sinners entice you, do not consent. If they say,
"Come with us, let us lie in wait to shed blood;
Let us lurk secretly for the innocent without cause;
let us swallow them alive . . .
We shall find all kinds of precious possessions,
we shall fill our houses with spoil;
cast in your lot among us, let us all have one purse" —
my son, do not walk in the way with them,
keep your foot from their path; for their feet run to evil,
and they make haste to shed blood.
Surely . . . they lie in wait for their own blood,
They lurk secretly for their own lives.
— Proverbs 1:8-18

Victor was just 13 years old when he joined the gang. He was small for his age, and said the reason he joined the gang was because they accepted him — small and all.

It wasn't long until the gang seemed like family to Victor, and soon he was deeply involved in all of the gang's activities — including some of the drive-by shootings. The gang proudly called Victor "their little gangster." But within months the little gangster was arrested. Victor is now serving a life sentence for murder.

The sad fact is that Victor is just one of an exploding number of young people joining gangs across America. In 1985 there were approximately 400 gangs in the greater Los Angeles area with a total membership of about 4,500 members. But in five short years the number of L.A. gangs had doubled to 800; membership had increased twenty-fold — to a whopping 90,000. And since that time, the L.A. gangs have not only continued to expand locally, but to spread east to escalate their recruiting in every major city of America.

When studying the phenomenal growth of gangs in the United States, the question arises, What makes a gang so attractive to American youth? And even more importantly, what keeps them involved in gang activity — even to the extent of great personal risk?

Those questions are best answered by remembering that every human being on earth has three inherent needs:

1. the need for significance;
2. the need for success; and
3. the need to belong.

Nobody wants to be a nobody. So if you're small, as Victor was . . . if you feel insignificant — join a gang. Because everybody would rather be a bad somebody than a nobody. We all want significance.

We also all want to be part of something that's "successful" — noticed . . . on the move . . . growing. We want to be part of and contribute to something that's "happening."

And we all want to belong. To be a part of "one for all and all for one." It's natural. We were never meant to go it alone. We were designed to identify with others.

Perhaps you recognize these words:

Sometimes you want to go where everybody
    knows your name
And they're always glad you came.
You want to be where you see your troubles are
    all the same.
You want to be where everybody knows your
    name.

They are the opening words of the hit TV show, "Cheers," filmed each week in a bar. You see, people hang out at bars for the same reason they join a gang.

They're lonely. They want to be accepted. To be important. Significant. Successful. To belong. And with a few drinks under your belt, you can be all those things — or at least feel you are — until the booze wears off.

But there's a better way — a more permanent way — to not just *feel* significant and successful and like you belong. There's a way to *be* significant . . . to *be* successful . . . and to *really belong.*

It's a God-given plan that began, oddly enough, with a baby's cry in a Bethlehem stable. But that plan finds its fulfillment now — or its death — with an important person — you. You can discover why with one simple turn of the page.

Let us lay aside the weight of individualism . . .
and let us run with endurance
the race that is set before us.
— based on Hebrews 12:1

17

WANTED: A NEW BODY

Therefore, when He [Jesus] came into the world,
He said: "Sacrifice and offering You did not desire,
but a body You have prepared for Me."
— Hebrews 10:5

To be significant. To be successful. To belong. That's exactly what God had in mind for all of His children. He wants us to have a sense of importance, of value. He wants us to be winners. And He has provided the opportunity for us to belong, forever.

That's why He created us in His own image. That's why He put us in a family. And that's why after man sinned, God formed His own family called the nation of Israel. He called Israel His redeemed people . . . the apple of His eye. He told the Israelites that He would not only be their God, but He would be their Father, and that they would share an intimate relationship.

Together they crossed the Red Sea and vast wilderness of Sinai. Together they crossed the Jordan River and conquered the Promised Land. God was with them. He was their Father. And because of Him, they enjoyed significance and success and a sense of belonging — to each other as well as to Him.

It was out of that family of Israel that God sent His

Son in the flesh. His name was Jesus Christ. He came down to our level — born in a human body . . . to live as man among men. He took on our likeness — a body of flesh and blood — so that He could understand our pressures . . . our humanity.

Everywhere Jesus went, He gave significance and value to those He touched. He let them know that they, too, could be winners. He showed them He was interested in them regardless of their sins. He gave them a sense of belonging as He told them they had a Heavenly Father who understood and was concerned about their needs — about things like food and clothing, health and happiness.

Then Jesus died on the cross. Faithful followers laid His body in a tomb. Three days later, Jesus rose again and ascended to heaven — bodily. He had completed His earthly ministry and went back to His Father's throne to share His Father's authority.

No longer was there a "body" on earth to show the world who God is and what He is like.

God needed a new "body" on earth that would express His love and demonstrate His power — one that would fill people's needs, give them significance, help them be successful, and most of all, provide a place to belong.

The Bible calls that new "body" — the new "body of Christ" — the church (1 Cor. 12:27; Eph. 4:11-16). Now the life of Jesus is lived out in that new body.

But not everyone is a member of that Body. As with every organization, there are membership requirements. The only way anyone becomes a member of the body of Christ — the church — is by accepting Jesus Christ as Saviour — believing that He died and rose again to pay the price for our sins.

But Christianity — being a member of the body of Christ — is far more than just a private transaction with God through Jesus Christ. It is that, for sure. But along with that private commitment to Jesus Christ comes an equally important commitment to the church. In fact, the two commitments are inseparable.

Remember when Simon Peter made his great confession of faith? It happened at Caesarea Philippi. Jesus asked His followers what people were saying about Him. The disciples answered that some people thought Jesus was John the Baptist or Elijah or Jeremiah or another one of the prophets.

Then Jesus asked, "Who do *you* say I am?" To which Peter replied, "You are the Christ, the Son of the living God" (Matt. 16:16).

Three cheers for Peter! He had just made that all-important commitment to faith in Jesus Christ.

But notice how Jesus responded. Jesus didn't say, "Peter, because you've confessed that I am the Christ, the Son of the living God, now you will have abundant life. Go in peace."

No. Jesus responded to Peter's confession by establishing the church:

> Jesus answered and said to him, "Blessed are you, Simon Bar-Jonah, for flesh and blood has not revealed this to you, but My Father who is in heaven. And I also say to you that you are Peter, and on this rock I will build My church, and the gates of Hades [death] shall not prevail against it" (Matt. 16:17-18).

Upon Peter's confession of faith, Jesus established a divine pattern that we also are to follow. When we confess Jesus Christ as our Saviour, then we also are to identify ourselves with His body, the church. We become part of His family. We become members of His church and our commitment is only to Jesus Christ. Our commitment is also to His body, the Church.

The fact is, you cannot make a commitment to Jesus Christ and be independent of or indifferent to His church.

The two are inseparable.

Remember Peter's sermon in Acts 2? Remember what Peter said when the crowd asked, "What shall we do?" Peter said,

> "Repent, and let every one of you be baptized in the name of Jesus Christ for the remission of sins; and you shall receive the gift of the Holy Spirit." . . . Then those who gladly received his word were baptized; and that day about three thousand souls were added to them" (Acts 2:38-41).

"Them" who? By reading on, we discover the 3,000 were added to the church:

> And they continued steadfastly in the apostles' doctrine and fellowship, in the breaking of bread, and in prayers. . . . And the Lord added to the church daily those who were being saved" (Acts 2:42-47).

Peter was saying that when we trust Christ, we should be baptized as an outward sign of an inward work of grace within our lives.

But also, Peter said when we trust Christ, the Holy Spirit baptizes us into the body of Christ and we become members of His church — His new body on earth.

Other Scriptures expand on this:

> For by one Spirit we were all baptized into one body. . . . But now indeed there are many members, yet one body. . . . Now you are the body of Christ, and members individually. And God has appointed these in the church (1 Cor. 12:13-28).

> There is one body and one Spirit . . . one Lord, one faith, one baptism; one God and Fa-

ther of all, who is above all, and through all, and
in you all (Eph. 4:4-6).

When we trust Jesus as Saviour, our commitment, then,
is not only to the Christ of the church; our commitment is
also to the church of Jesus Christ.

Why? Because it is in that body — and through that
body — that God desires to meet the needs of mankind.
The need for significance. The need for success. The need
to belong.

And it works — as long as the members of that body
are free of the debilitating weight of individualism. For a
look at its earliest warning signs, read on.

Let us lay aside the weight of individualism . . .
and let us run with endurance
the race that is set before us.
— based on Hebrews 12:1

18

INTER-DEPENDENCE DAY

But God composed the body . . .
that there should be no schism in the body,
but that the members
should have the same care for one another.
— 1 Corinthians 12:24-25

It's the proverbial monkey wrench. It's Murphy's Law. Everything running smoothly, until. . . . If that's the story of your plans . . . your life, take heart. You're not alone. That's been the story of some of God's plans as well.

Take the Garden of Eden, for instance. It was the perfect place for man to live — paradise on earth. Everything paid for and provided. Adam and Eve were innocent and enjoyed it all. Until. . . .

It happens every time someone begins focusing too hard or too closely or too often on one's self . . . when "I" begin believing and acting as if my interests — what *I want* — outweighs the interests of everyone else.

In Eden, Satan tempted Eve to put her interests — what she wanted — above what God wanted.

And in the church today, there's still that same temptation — and still too many Eves and too many Adams. So many, in fact, that in a survey of people asked to name the heaviest "weights" slowing down Christians today, "individualism" ranked in the top ten.

It was called by its other names — selfishness . . . dissension . . . disunity. It's the thing that turns long-time members into drop-outs or church-splitters. It's the thing that visitors call unfriendliness; the hypocrisy that keeps outsiders away permanently.

In short, individualism is the number one obstacle that keeps people from having their needs met by the church in the way that God intended.

And no wonder. Individualism was the sin of Satan that preceded his lightning-like fall from heaven (Luke 10:18). You see, Satan — or Lucifer, as he was called back then — became dissatisfied with being the anointed cherub who covered the heavenly throne (Ezek. 28:14). He began focusing on what *he* wanted rather than on what *God* wanted (Isa. 14:12-17).

And he has made a habit of encouraging human recruits to his doctrine of individualism ever since.

They're often found in church pews on Sunday morning. You can recognize them by the way they mutter things under their breath during the service. Or by what they try to stir up in the hallways or restrooms between times.

They say things like, "Well, I guess how *I* feel just isn't important to this church anymore." Or, "I sure wish they'd spend that much money on something *I'm* interested in." "Why can't we have the kind of music *I* like?" "How come they're recognizing them — and not *me*?" "*I've given* as much to this place as anybody." And on and on and on.

Maybe it's to be expected. After all, we are the "Me" generation . . . a consumer society . . . used to having whatever we want — now!

But worst of all, it's very possible that we are the generation who will fulfill this damning end-time prophecy:

> But know this, that in the last days perilous
> times will come: For men will be lovers of them-

selves, lovers of money, boasters, proud, blasphemers, disobedient to parents, unthankful, unholy, unloving, unforgiving, slanderers, without self-control, brutal, despisers of good, traitors, headstrong, haughty, lovers of pleasure rather than lovers of God, having a form of godliness but denying its power (2 Tim. 3:1-5).

A while back *USA Today* surveyed church-goers. Forty-five percent said that the reason they go to church is because it makes them feel good. Another 26 percent said they went because it gives them peace of mind and a spiritual feeling of well-being.

Now there's nothing wrong with people feeling good after going to church. They should. That's the point, remember? Finding significance and success and a sense of belonging is what church is all about.

But if "feeling good" is the only reason you are going to church, you are probably an overweight individualist expecting a warm fuzzy in exchange for your religiosity. You're a getter, not a giver.

Have you checked out the bookstore lately? Do you know what's hot? Books that deal with self-esteem, self-fulfillment, self-analysis . . . while the books about sacrifice and commitment are gathering dust on those same shelves.

The point is that while God longs to use individuals, He has real difficulty using an individualist.

An individual is a person with his or her own unique personality and gifts. Individuals are what make the body of Christ unique.

An individualist is someone who either can't or who doesn't want to relate to someone else.

Individualists make poor packages because they are all wrapped up in themselves.

An individualist wants independence — total freedom from everyone else — to be exempt from the control as well as the support of others.

Individualists have an attitude. I can make it on my own. I can do it myself. You run your race; I'll run mine. Don't call me; I'll call you. I want to be free to live my life the way I want . . . to do what I want to do when I want to do it . . . to be my own ultimate authority.

It translates into isolation — non-participation in the body of Christ, the church.

And that's why gangs are growing like — well, gangbusters; and the church, in many cases, is not.

So what's the answer? The Bible says it's interdependence.

That's how becoming a Christian begins in the first place. I depend on God to forgive my sins through Christ's death on the cross. And the moment that happened, I became a member of Christ's body, the church. As a member, I'm depending on God, but I'm also depending on you. And hoping that you are depending on God as well.

I lose my independence to depend on God and others. I am still an individual, but have set aside my individualistic tendencies. I make a commitment . . . and I follow through.

Together, we have significance . . . find success . . . and enjoy a sense of belonging — to God and to each other.

That's the challenge the apostle Paul put before the first century church at Rome. And it's the challenge God still sets before the church today:

> I beseech you therefore, brethren, by the mercies of God, that you present your bodies a living sacrifice, holy, acceptable to God, which is your reasonable service.

> And do not be conformed to this world, but be transformed by the renewing of your mind, that you may prove what is that good and acceptable and perfect will of God.

> For I say, through the grace given to me, to

everyone who is among you, not to think of himself more highly than he ought to think, but to think soberly, as God has dealt to each one a measure of faith.

For as we have many members in one body, but all the members do not have the same function, so we, being many, are one body in Christ, and individually members of one another.

Having then gifts differing according to the grace that is given to us, let us use them. . . .

Be kindly affectionate to one another with brotherly love, in honor giving preference to one another (Rom. 12:1-10).

In honor giving preference to one another. That pretty much sums it up. The opposite of individualism.

It's God's goal for the Church — Christ's body on earth. It begins with setting aside all selfish weights and making a commitment to Jesus Christ and His church.

A good way to do that right now is by offering Him this simple prayer:

Dear Jesus,
   I confess you as my Lord, and I now
   commit by Your grace to help build Your church.
Lord Jesus,
   You can count on me to do whatever
   I can to strengthen Your body
   and I thank You for the opportunity.
In Christ's name, I pray, amen.

Let us lay aside the weight of individualism . . .
and let us run with endurance
the race that is set before us.
— based on Hebrews 12:1

PART 6
LET US LAY ASIDE THE WEIGHT OF INDIVIDUALISM

Individualism: an egotistical mentality that puts individual interests above those of the whole.

While God loves and respects each person as an individual, and while each person is held individually accountable, the spirit of individual-*ism* is contrary to God's nature as well as His plan for man.

Man has, within his nature, three genuine desires that are best fulfilled in a family or community atmosphere: (1) the need to be significant, (2) the need to be successful, and (3) the need to belong.

Satan has capitalized on these desires through the ages, and is today meeting those needs in our children and youth through an unprecedented growth in gangs.

On the other hand, more and more churches are doing just the opposite — *failing* to meet those needs — *failing* to keep children and youth involved . . . and *failing* to meet the felt needs of the membership at large.

Instead of individuals feeling a sense of belonging . . . instead of them experiencing significance and success within the church setting, more and more Christians are feeling less and less commitment, not only to the Lord *but to each other.*

The weight of individualism is pervading the church in America today, keeping it and its members from running the race that God has set before us in these last days.

DAY 1

TODAY'S DIET: John 10:30; 17:20-23; 1 John 5:7
EXERCISE: God's very nature decries the spirit of individualism. While God is a triune being — three individuals — God the Father, God the Son, and God the Holy Spirit, He is one. And although each member of the trinity has a specific office and performs specific duties, at no time is

the action of one member of the trinity individualistic — selfish, independent, isolated, uncomplimentary, or detrimental to the actions of either of the others. Their work is intricately interrelated and inter-dependent to achieve eternal goals.

• Read the following Scriptures and note the individual work of the members of the trinity mentioned in each passage. Then notice how each one's work is interrelated to the others'.

Matthew 26:39	John 5:19	John 6:44	John 8:29
John 2:49,50	John 14:26	John 15:26	John 17:5

• In John 17:20-23, Jesus prays that all who believe on Him will become one as He and the Father are one. What do you think He meant?

_____
_____
_____

• Do you feel as if you are "one" with other Christians? If not, why do you think that is?

• Pray about your involvement with other Christians. Ask the Lord to reveal to you if you are carrying, perhaps unknowingly, a weight of individualism — putting *yourself*, *your* desires and *your* needs above others.

DAY 2

TODAY'S DIET: Genesis 2:18-24; 29:12-14; Mark 10:6-9
EXERCISE: Creation decries the spirit of individualism. Read Genesis 1:26. When God said, "Let **Us** make man in **Our** image, who was He talking about? _____

_____

• After God created man, He said, "It is not good that man should be alone; I will make him a helper comparable to him" (Gen. 2:18).

> If you have not already read Genesis 2:18-24, do so now. How does this passage contradict the idea of individualism?
>
> How does it support the idea that God never intended for man to go it alone?
>
> How do you see God supplying the needs of man for significance, success and a sense of belonging?

• God intended for our families to meet our needs. Think about your family members. Are any individualistic? Are you?

• If you are living with family, consider the following:

> How many times per week does your family eat together?
>
> Does each family member have assigned tasks that are beneficial to other members of the family?
>
> When watching television, do you watch it as a family, or do some members routinely watch it in a separate room?

• If you are not living with family, consider:

> How many times a week do you talk to or see family?
>
> Do you initiate those times, or does someone else?
>
> If a family member calls or wants to get together, do you feel it is more of an imposition or more of a joy?

• Pray, asking the Lord to show you how your family can be more as He would have it be. In the Bible, when Laban met his nephew Jacob for the first time, Laban said, "Surely you are my bone and my flesh" (Gen. 29:14). Ask the Lord to help you genuinely feel and act similarly with all the members of your family.

DAY 3

TODAY'S DIET: Psalm 68:5-6; John 1:11-12; 1 John 3:1-2; Romans 8:15-17

EXERCISE: It is not surprising that God likens the relationship of believers and God to that of an earthly family. After all, the main characteristic of an earthly family should be love; and the determining factor of God's family is His love that reached out and provided for sinful man.

• Re-read Psalm 68:5-6.

> Think about how these verses might apply to God's provision for believers within a local church family.
>
> Do you see an application in these verses with regard to the need for significance? For success? For a sense of belonging?

• The way God sets "the solitary" in His family is outlined in the other Scriptures in today's "diet." If you are unsure about whether you are a part of God's family, re-read those verses carefully and study Romans 10:9-10 and Acts 16:31.

• If you know that you are a child of God but feel isolated from the rest of the family of God, ask the Lord to show you if those feelings stem from self-imposed isolation and independence — from a spirit of individualism. Ask yourself:

> How many times per month do I attend a worship service?
>
> Am I actively involved in at least one small group?
>
> How much do I know about those I see and sit with?
>
> Am I part of an information network; i.e., if someone is sick, how quickly do I hear about it?

When there is a need, how quickly do I respond?

When I respond, is it in a personal way (helping to provide a meal for the family, for instance) or is it more detached (sending a card with little or no more follow-up)?

Do I expect more from other members in the church than I, myself, am willing to give?

• After honest, prayerful assessment, begin to take steps this week to counteract any symptoms of individualism you are experiencing.

• Consider what steps you can take to help others who seem isolated to feel as though they, too, are part of God's family.

• Outline ways that you can help first-time visitors graduate to become active, involved members of church themselves.

DAY 4

TODAY'S DIET: Romans 12

EXERCISE: Losing the weight of individualism and keeping it off requires discipline and persistence. The apostle Paul addressed the problem in his letter to the first century church at Rome. While you may know Romans 12:1-2 by heart, you may not have ever realized that those verses are actually an introduction to Paul's lecture against individualism! In verses 3 through 5, Paul says, "Don't be individualistic." Compare those verses with the definition of individualism at the beginning of this study guide. Now back up to verses 1 and 2. Notice that:

Losing the weight of individualism is only possible *"by the mercies of God."*

It requires more than a change of attitude; it requires physical activity — "present your bodies . . . which is your reasonable service."

> Losing the weight of individualism and keeping it off is a day-to-day part of living; and it is hard: "present your bodies a living *sacrifice*."
>
> It is contrary to the spirit of the age and the worldly encouragement to do your own thing: "Do not be conformed to this world but be transformed by the renewing of your mind."
>
> It is *"good and acceptable"* and fulfills *"the perfect will of God."*

• Romans 12:6 tells us that each individual has "gifts" and that we are to "use them." Are you using your gifts to bless others in a local church? If not, why not?

• In verses 9 through 21, many other practical ways of dealing with and defeating individualism are given. On a separate sheet of paper, list five you will strive to focus on in the coming weeks.

DAY 5

TODAY'S DIET: Proverbs 1:8-19

EXERCISE: God created man with three genuine desires: the need for significance, the need to succeed, and the need to belong. Today, Satan offers the fulfillment of those desires in children and youth through gangs. Three thousand years ago, parents warned about gangs. Use Proverbs 1:8-19 as a basis for discussion about gangs with your own children and others.

Discuss the fact that gang activity is not anything new. Compare what gangs offer today with the description given in Proverbs. Point out the relevancy of God's Word for today. Talk about the three basic appeals of a gang: (1) power [the need for significance], (2) money [the need for success], and (3) friendship, or a sense of family [the need to belong].

Discover together how God intended that mankind's desires find fulfillment, first of all, in a human family; and secondly later, in *His* family, the church.

• God intended that the needs of individuals be met in His church by believers. And He intended that His people and His church be characterized by a spirit of *one-ness* and a sense of *one-anotherness,* the opposite of individualism. Read the following "one another" verses and discover how God intended for us to lay aside the heavy weight of individualism:

Mark 9:50 _____

John 13:34 _____

Romans 12:10 _____

Romans 15:7 _____

Galatians 5:13 _____

Ephesians 4:32 _____

Ephesians 5:21 _____

1 Thessalonians 5:11 _____

James 5:9 _____

James 5:16 _____

1 Peter 5:5 _____

19

THE TIME TRAP

For man also does not know his time:
Like fish taken in a cruel net, like birds caught in a snare,
so the sons of men are snared in an evil time,
when it falls suddenly upon them.
— Ecclesiastes 9:12

Take a moment to flip back through the first few chapters of this book. As you do, you will recall that those chapters began with a look at the gold and silver vessels that were used to serve God in the tabernacle and temple. As we examined those vessels, we discovered that they were prepared by weight — a prescribed weight that was determined by God himself.

We also discovered that since there is no longer a tabernacle or temple with gold and silver bowls and platters and spoons, that God has chosen in our time to use another kind of vessel in His service — *us* — according to 2 Corinthians 4:7.

As God's chosen vessels, we, too, are to be a God-prescribed weight spiritually speaking (Prov. 16:2; Job 31:6). Not *under*weight — lacking things that God intends and expects us to have; and not *over*weight — unduly heavy with cares, concerns, habits, or problems — that slow us down.

In the previous chapters, we have examined some of

those weights — frustration, guilt, financial pressure, individualism. Plus, we've noted that "the race" — the Christian life — is not a sprint and not a 50-yard dash. It's a
grueling marathon, requiring strength, flexibility, and discipline in order to run — and complete it — victoriously.

In this section we will focus on another aspect of the
race — one summed up by a single word in the theme verse
— the word, *endurance*:

> Let us lay aside every weight and let us run
> with *endurance* the race that is set before us (Heb.
> 12:1).

According to *The New Webster's Encyclopedic Dictionary of the English Language,* the word *endurance* means
"the capacity to keep going or to put up with pain, hardship, etc., *for a long time"* [emphasis added].

When God's Holy Spirit inspired the author to write
Hebrews 12:1, His thought must have been, *I want everyone to understand by My very selection of the word, endurance, that the Christian life — the "race" — is going to
require some **time**.*

And yet, in a survey of hundreds of people, asked what
they felt were the top three weights hindering Christians in
America today, the "lack of time" ranked number two.

That means that the very thing that God said is required to run a successful spiritual race — time — is in
critically short supply.

In the survey people said things like, "I'm just too
busy." "Life is more hectic now than it's ever been before."
Or the classic and often repeated cliché, "There aren't
enough hours in the day."

We're too busy to get things in the mail on time, so we
overnight them. We don't have time to gift-wrap anymore,
so we gift-sack — stashing last-minute purchases and col-
ored tissue paper in glorified shopping bags.

We've replaced multi-tasking with giga-tasking. Our

daytimers are now day-*and-night*-timers. We've increased the speed limit on many highways from 55 to 65 and even 75 mph in some places.

We buy groceries in quantities of 15 items or less so we can go through the express lane. Or we dash into the 24-hour convenience store at the 23rd hour.

We phone on the run — even eat on the run. In fact, did you know that the home-cooked pot roast is now on the endangered species list of America?

The number one answer to the question, "How are you?" is now, "Busy!" But isn't it interesting that people are never too busy to tell you how busy they are?

The fact is, the most common complaint of our time is that we have *no* time. Not for our families, not for ourselves; not even for church or God.

That translates into disaster, spiritually speaking. Instead of seeing disciplined, paced, determined, focused, spiritual athletes, we are seeing more and more hectic, harried, hurried racers.

Racers who swap lanes indiscriminately. Racers who run with occasional enthusiastic bursts of energy only to collapse periodically on the sidelines, red-faced, panting, and discouraged. Racers who feel that if they just had a little more time, they could do a much better job of living the Christian life.

But would we? Chances are that even if we had more time, we'd treat it exactly as we already treat the 24 hours God gives us each day. Perhaps worse.

Do you know that each year, some pediatricians mark their calendars with a big red X on the day when Daylight Saving Time begins? Do you know why?

It's because Daylight Saving Time means more outdoor playing time for children, and less indoor, quieter time. And that means more injuries.

Sadly, unless things change dramatically in most of *our* lives, even if we were given more time, we would do exactly what the children do. We would pack it full of more activity . . . more busy-ness . . . rather than reserving it for *less* activity and *more quiet time* with God.

How foolish we are! Especially when the Bible tells us that when we spend time obediently focusing on the things of God, He rewards us with the very thing so many of us say we lack — *time, itself:*

> My son, do not forget my law, but let your heart keep my commands; for length of days and long life and peace they will add to you (Prov. 3:1-2).

> The fear of the Lord is the beginning of wisdom, and the knowledge of the Holy One is understanding. For by me your days will be multiplied, and years of life will be added to you (Prov. 9:10-11).

> The fear of the Lord prolongs days, but the years of the wicked will be shortened (Prov. 10:27).

After all, *eternal* time — perpetual life — is the ultimate benefit of our salvation!

So what has gone wrong with our time management skills? Where do the hours go? And who do they really belong to?

Why are we seeing so little of God and so little of the things of God on the race track? The answer lies in the pages ahead.

Let us lay aside the weight of the lack of time . . .
and let us run with endurance
the race that is set before us.
— based on Hebrews 12:1

20

TIME FRAMED

Surely every man walks about like a shadow;
Surely they busy themselves in vain.
— Psalm 39:6

It's a problem a man named Job pondered centuries ago: Where does time go? And why do we have so little of it to spend on the good things of life?

Job said:

My days are swifter than a weaver's shuttle (Job 7:6).

Swifter than a runner; They flee away, they see no good. They pass by like swift ships, Like an eagle swooping on its prey (Job 9:25-26).

Since times are not hidden from the Almighty, Why do those who know Him see not His days? (Job 24:1).

If God sets a race before us that requires time, why has the *lack* of time become the very weight hindering us from running the race victoriously?

If you're like most Americans, you've probably seen a hundred articles on time management. You've probably tried scheduling and priority lists, mental or otherwise, only to be frustrated by the interruptions — the time-stealers — of the day. And we all are well-acquainted with the overwhelming feeling of having "so much to do, and so little time to do it."

The question is, Why? The answer unfolds with a look back at the beginning of time.

You see, time is not a creation of man; it's a creation of God. He is the One who set the earth spinning on its axis to form day and night. He is the One who hung the lights in the sky and said, "Let them be for signs and season, weeks and years" (Gen. 1:14). God is the One who originally gave man the gift of time.

Therefore, it stands to reason that effective, successful time management requires more than a few basic principles taught by secular time management experts. It takes more than just discipline or organization or utilization of a few tricks or tips. Those are good, and you ought to make them part of your life.

But when we realize that as believers, life is a spiritual marathon where every moment counts, and where we are accountable for every moment, secular principles fall far short of the help we need.

Successful time management requires *spiritual* understanding, *spiritual* power, and *spiritual* intervention.

The first thing we need to understand is:

WHO OUR TIME REALLY BELONGS TO

Most of us believe it belongs to God — but act like it belongs to us.

The truth is that while God created time *for* man, and allocates time *to* man, our time is really under a powerful evil influence that affects every productive period of our day.

Ephesians 5:16 says it this way: "The days are evil."

Two words are especially interesting in that verse. They

are the original Greek words, the first of which is translated, *"days."* The second one is translated, *"evil."*

The Greek word for "days" literally means *"the time space between dawn and dark."* That's our productive time. The second Greek word, translated, "evil," refers to a *bad influence* that already affects each day before it ever pops up on the calendar.

Our days from sunrise to sunset are predisposed to evil things. They invite trouble. In fact, they welcome it. By their very nature they attract everything bad — hard work, annoyances, hardships, harassment's, pressure, peril, pain, and trouble. It's a pre-packaged deal. It's — well, "life."

But all of this doesn't mean that time itself is evil. It couldn't be. It was created and given to man by God.

What it does mean is that something has corrupted God's gift of time to the point that each morning you wake up, the hours ahead are already infected . . . diseased . . . destined for worthlessness. The day that you desire to use *pro*-ductively is already claimed to be used *de*-structively by the forces of evil.

Notice that the Bible does not say, "There *may* be *some* evil in your day." Or, "There'll be good days and bad days." The Bible says, "The days *are evil"* — all of them. Your time has been framed and imprisoned . . . the victim of a wicked conspiracy.

Does that sound like something God would be involved in? Of course not.

First John 1:5 says:

God is light, and in Him is no darkness at all.

And Psalm 5:4 declares,

For You are not a God who takes pleasure in wickedness, Nor shall evil dwell with You.

Therefore we must conclude that the evil influencing our days does not come from God. It doesn't even come from us. Rather, our days are at the mercy of the evil influence of the evil one, Satan himself.

That's why the apostle Paul wrote these words:

> But the Lord is faithful, who will establish you and guard you from the evil one. And we have confidence in the Lord concerning you, both that you do and will do the things we command you (2 Thess. 3:3-4).

Paul knew that effective time management — doing the things we want and need to do — depends on victory over Satan and his evil designs to ruin our time. And that begins with the stark realization that the days are evil.

The second thing we need to understand is:

HOW OUR TIME GOT SO MESSED UP

The answer can be summed up in four small words: the fall of man.

When Adam and Eve sinned, it affected more than their relationship with God. Everything earthly was instantly altered — including time.

Suddenly evil would have an icy choke-hold on the hours between dawn and dusk for centuries to come. It was a subtle grip coming in the form of interruptions and infringements mankind had never known before.

Prior to the fall, "work" was a hobby. After the fall, it became hard, time-consuming, sweat-producing labor necessary for survival. Instead of the ground willingly yielding its fruit as it had in Eden, the soil grudgingly guarded its produce, clasping it tightly among the thorns and thistles.

Sunburn and muscle aches, pains and strains all became a part of an ordinary day. Man discovered his own physical weakness — and how exhaustion, a common cold, or the flu could cut into time and wreck already-too-tight schedules.

His once-perfect mind now forgot things — forcing

him to retrace his steps . . . re-book appointments . . . re-work reports.

Things broke, got lost, stolen.

Temptations of all kinds began begging for their own share of time-wasting attention.

Emotions surged. Jealousy. Greed. Pride. People began having problems with family, friends, and co-workers. Time out for conflict management became a daily must for everyone — from mothers refereeing sibling rivalry to executives mediating personnel problems and policy.

Adam died. Eve died. Abel was killed. The reality of being mortal set in. Life suddenly seemed too short — and too stressful — to get everything done before it was over.

Time was under attack. Productivity was threatened. Evil was taking over from the moment the sun rose in the east to the second it set in the west.

And for the first time since time began, *time itself* and the *lack of time* became a weight for all mankind.

The good news is that God never leaves us stranded. Not even when we've messed up His gift of time in a beautiful garden.

He never tells us to lay aside a weight that's too heavy to lift. Instead, He lays out a plan for losing it forever. And fortunately, that plan is just seconds — and one thin page — away.

Let us lay aside the weight of the lack of time . . .
and let us run with endurance
the race that is set before us.
— based on Hebrews 12:1

21

GIMME JUST A SECOND

A wise man's heart discerns both time and judgment.
— Ecclesiastes 8:5

The wonderful thing about the Bible is that it never raises a question without giving the answer. It never points out a problem without giving the solution.

The particular problem we're talking about is found in Ephesians 5:16: "The days are evil." Our time between dawn and dark is predestined for worthlessness . . . for a variety of interruptions each infringing on the things we hoped to accomplish for the day.

That's the problem. But the answer is there, too — in the very same verse. And explained in the verse before and the verse after:

> See then that you walk circumspectly
> [shrewdly], not as fools but as wise, **redeeming**
> **the time**, because the days are evil. Therefore do
> not be unwise, but understand what the will of
> the Lord is (Eph. 5:15-17).

That's the answer. Redeeming the time. "Buying back" what evil possessed. Changing the predisposition of our days. Thwarting bad before it begins. Watching out for it and shrewdly challenging it, all day long. Redeeming, buying back, what God gave us in the first place.

The doctrine of redemption is a wonderful theme of the New Testament. Over and over again we're told that God sent His Son to redeem fallen man — to buy him back by paying man's penalty for sin:

> But when the fullness of the time was come, God sent forth His Son, born of a woman, made under the law, To redeem those who were under the law, that we might receive the adoption of sons (Gal. 4:4-5).

> Looking for that blessed hope, and the glorious appearing of the great God and our Saviour Jesus Christ; Who gave himself for us, that he might redeem us from all iniquity (Titus 2:13-14;KJV).

Just as sinful man can be redeemed, redeemed man can buy back evil days. Time, destined for worthlessness can be reclaimed for worthwhileness. The day that the forces of evil plan to use for *de*-struction can be bought back and used for *pro*-duction — if you know how.

In the last chapter you read the statement that proper time management requires more than basic time management principles. More than discipline. More than organization. More than the utilization of a few key tricks or tips. All of those things are good, but too often we discover they're ineffective. We slip back into the same old patterns and wind up with the same old problem — too much to do and too little time to do it.

But when you couple all the best secular time management strategies with *spiritual* understanding, *spiritual* power, and *spiritual* intervention, you develop a time management program guaranteed to rescue every waking hour of every single day from the influence of evil.

You're over the first hurdle — spiritual understanding — when you come to grips with the fact that the days are evil and that time management is actually spiritual warfare.

STEP #1: UNDERSTAND THAT THE DAYS ARE EVIL AND THAT EACH ONE MUST BE REDEEMED.

Satan would like you to believe something different. He would like you to believe that your problem with time — or the lack of it — is *your* fault — *all* your fault.

That's his job. To lie to you. To deceive you. To steal your time. To kill your efficiency. To defeat your effectiveness. To destroy your dreams . . . your joy . . . your sense of fulfillment. To keep you from crossing the finish line, fit and trim. God does just the opposite:

> The devil . . . does not stand in the truth, because there is no truth in him. When he speaks a lie, he speaks from his own resources, for he is a liar and the father of it (John 8:44).

> The great dragon . . . that serpent of old, called the Devil and Satan . . . deceives the whole world (Rev. 12:9).

> The thief does not come except to steal, and to kill, and to destroy. I [Jesus] have come that they may have life, and that they may have it more abundantly (John 10:10).

Each day when you wake up, you have a choice. You can either engage your spiritual understanding and commit to buy back the day from evil; or you can disregard God's warning in Ephesians 5 and let the time from dawn till dusk slip uselessly into the tomb of time.

Should you choose the path of spiritual understanding, your next step involves activating spiritual power to deal with whatever evil the day throws at you.

STEP #2: POWER UP WITH PRAYER AND BIBLE STUDY.

Jesus did. And if He needed to, how much more do

we? It appears that Jesus began each day with prayer to reclaim it from evil for good and for God.

> Now in the morning, having risen a long while before daylight, He went out and departed to a solitary place; and there He prayed (Mark 1:35).

On one occasion when Jesus had concluded His prayer time, one of the disciples went to him with the request, "Teach us to pray" (Luke 11:1). Notice that the disciple didn't say, "Teach us *how* to pray"; but "Teach us *to* pray."

No doubt he had seen how much Jesus got done in a day — multitudes taught, critics refuted, blind and lame and sick and deaf all healed. And yet, the disciples noticed, Jesus always seemed to have time left over to answer their questions, to notice a fruitless fig tree beside the road, to hold children on his lap, to meet friends for dinner.

And He did it stress free. No wrinkled forehead or splitting headache. He never made anyone feel like they were taking His valuable time. He never snapped a thoughtless or hasty answer at a single person.

The secret, the disciples discovered, lay to a large extent in Jesus' consistent, early morning prayer life. He joined ranks with the Father and battled in prayer to redeem the day before dawn ever came.

When Jesus responded to the disciple's request, "Teach us to pray," He did so by giving what we call the Lord's Prayer or the Model Prayer. You probably remember how it begins:

> Our Father who art in heaven, hallowed be Thy name. . . .

But do you remember how it ends? It ends with a plea for the day:

> And lead us not into temptation, but deliver us from evil: For Thine is the kingdom, and the power, and the glory, forever. Amen (Matt. 6:13).

Jesus knew that each day belonged to evil. He also knew that the temptation each day would be to let evil have it.

That's easier than fighting to buy back time, minute by minute, hour by hour, day after day. It requires deliverance from a blasé attitude. It requires the power of God at work in our lives. And that power is tapped through prayer.

Jesus also knew from personal experience that evil bows to the authority of the Scriptures. You probably remember the incident recorded in Matthew 4. Jesus has fasted 40 days and 40 nights. No doubt He was weak and vulnerable, physically speaking. But armed with the Word of God, He was empowered to defeat and drive off the evil consequences Satan had planned for that fateful day.

Three times Satan attacked, offering everything from food to fame, if Jesus would just sideline His mission momentarily. Each time, Jesus countered Satan's offers by quoting Scripture. Each time, Jesus redeemed the moment — bought it back from evil — by rehearsing passages from the Bible He had previously mastered.

The same method will work for you. Three good verses to pack in your daily redemption kit include:

> Being confident of this very thing, that He who has begun a good work in you will complete it until the day of Jesus Christ (Phil. 1:6).

> I can do all things through Christ who strengthens me (Phil. 4:13).

> Now to Him who is able to do exceedingly abundantly above all that we ask or think, according to the power that works in us, to Him be glory . . . by Christ Jesus throughout all ages, world without end (Eph. 3:20-21).

Effective time management for the Christian begins with spiritual understanding.

But it is empowered through daily prayer and Bible

study. And finally, effective time management requires spiritual discernment and intervention:

STEP #3: EVALUATE INTERRUPTIONS, DISTRACTIONS, AND DIVERSIONS TO DISCERN WHETHER THEY ARE DIVINE APPOINTMENTS OR JUST THE EVIL OF THE DAY RE-SURFACING.

That's what Jesus did. Sometimes the things that disrupted His schedule were orchestrated by God for a specific purpose. They were divine appointments, and had Jesus not recognized them as such, He would have missed God-given opportunities to bless and be blessed.

One time Jairus, an important ruler of the Jews, came to Jesus. His daughter was dying, and Jairus wanted Jesus to heal her. Along the way, a woman who had been ill for 12 years worked her way through the crowd surrounding Jesus. The woman believed that if she could just touch the hem of Jesus' robe, she would be healed. She did. And she was.

Jesus stopped. He didn't have to. The woman was healed. And the little girl was dying. But Jesus stopped anyway. He took time to recognize the woman — to look her in the eyes . . . to affirm and bless her.

In the meantime, a runner came from Jairus' house. There was no point in Jesus coming, he said. Jairus' daughter no longer needed to be healed. She had died.

But Jesus went anyway . . . and raised her from the dead. The interruption of the woman had been a divine appointment. For not only was she healed, but the crowd soon knew that Jesus was more than the Great Physician. He was God — with power over death as well as life (Luke 8:40-56).

Other times the interruptions were not so innocent . . . not divine at all . . . but evil, attempting to resurface and overtake the day.

We find one example in the Book of Mark. Jesus and the disciples had spent some time ministering in Capernaum prior to this particular occurrence. And it just so happens that this incident occurred right after Jesus had spent the pre-dawn hours in prayer. Notice what happened:

> Now in the morning, having risen a long while before daylight, He went out and departed to a solitary place; and there He prayed.
> And Simon and those who were with Him searched for Him. When they found Him, they said to Him, "Everyone is looking for You."
> But He said to them, "Let us go into the next towns, that I may preach there also, because for this purpose I have come forth" (Mark 1:35-38).

Jesus knew His mission. He had already submitted His "Things to Do" list to the Heavenly Father in prayer, and together they had agreed on the day's agenda.

So when everyone came looking for Jesus, begging Him to stay on in Capernaum, He was able to remain focused on His goal. He kept the interruption to a minimum and did not allow it to shift His attention or activity with regard to His goal.

That's a good plan of action for all of us.

First of all, outline your day during your morning prayer time. Whenever things begin to deviate from that plan, try to determine whether the changes are divine appointments or evil attempting to reclaim the day.

Some good questions to ask are:

> Will this interruption assist or hinder me in meeting my current goal?
> Which can wait with the least amount of damage — the goal or the interruption?
> Is there a relationship at stake?

Sometimes a backward look over the previous day will prepare you to face the evil of the upcoming day. Ask yourself:

Was any part of my day today affected by evil?

Why was I unable to redeem it?

What can I do differently from now on?

The bottom line is that we no longer have to be at the mercy of time that's controlled by the evil one. We can reclaim each day — one day at a time — for God's glory and for our good.

We no longer have to beg, "Gimme just a second" — because God has given us a second chance.

After all his trials and all his pondering about time on earth, Job wrote:

Behold, God is mighty, but despises no one; He is mighty in strength of understanding (Job 36:5).

He does not withdraw His eyes from the righteous; but they are on the throne with kings, for He has seated them forever, and they are exalted (Job 36:7).

If they obey and serve Him, they shall spend their days in prosperity, and their years in pleasure" (Job 36:11).

Days of prosperity. Years of pleasure. That's the kind of life we all want. And it's possible — when we obey and serve Him. When we redeem each day from the evil that threatens to ruin our race.

Let us lay aside the weight of the lack of time . . .
and let us run with endurance
the race that is set before us.
— based on Hebrews 12:1

PART 7
LET US LAY ASIDE THE WEIGHT
OF THE LACK OF TIME

Hebrews 12:1 encourages us to lay aside every weight that hinders us from running the race that God has set before us.

Hundreds of people were surveyed and asked to name the top three "weights" they felt were hindering Christians in America today. The number two answer was "the lack of time."

If you often feel like there is too much to do and too little time to do it — or know someone else feeling that way — follow this week's Scripture diet and exercise plan, and begin to lay that weight aside!

DAY 1

Today's Diet: Ecclesiastes 3:1-8, 17; 8:5-6; 2 Corinthians 5:10

Exercise: Christians burdened with a lack of time suffer personally, their families suffer; and Christ's church suffers, too. After hearing the accompanying message, and after reading today's Scripture passages, how would you counsel the following people?

"I used to come to Sunday night services all the time. But I hardly ever see my family as it is. We've reserved Sunday nights to do something special — watching a movie together . . . or playing a game."

"I would help with a kids' class at church, but I'm not sure what all it involves. I can see myself giving up a couple of hours on Sunday mornings, but I'm just too busy to check on the little urchins during the week as well. And if it involves any kind of training sessions, you can forget it, for sure!"

"I'm so tired of hearing the church needs volunteers for stuffing bulletins, cleaning the grounds, working on mailings, helping with the remodeling, and so on and so on and so on. Don't they know people already have more than they can handle? Why don't they hire the help they need and quit begging?!"

"I would love to sponsor a home group. But I would be embarrassed for anyone to see the way my house looks. I haven't had time to really clean it in I-don't-know-how-many weeks!"

DAY 2

Today's Diet: Isaiah 58:13-14; Romans 15:1-4; Hebrews 10:23-25
Exercise: Under the law of Moses, the Jews were required to honor God by devoting a block of time solely to Him. That block of time amounted to one-seventh of every week and was called the Sabbath. On the Sabbath, normal activities — especially work — stopped and the people gathered together in a holy assembly.

• Although we are not required to keep the Sabbath, the principle of honoring God with a block of our time is still valid. What types of things do you take time for each week to honor God? Be sure to consider Bible reading, prayer time, time spent in Bible study groups and church services, and time spent serving others in ministry.

_____

_____

_____

How many total hours per week do these activities involve?____ The Jews were required to honor God with one-seventh or about 14 percent of their time. What percentage of your total time do you give God? Divide the hours on the previous line by the total number of hours per week (168) to get your percentage: _____

How does your percentage compare? Do you think God expects us to spend more time, less time, or about the same amount of time honoring Him as He required from the Jews?

❑ more time   ❑ less time   ❑ about the same

• God intended that the time we spend honoring Him be "a delight" according to today's Isaiah passage. Do you find that to be true in your life? If not, perhaps your attitude toward God's time has become a weight that needs to be shed.

• God also intended that the time we spend honoring Him be good for us in other ways. Refer to today's passage in Hebrews and name some of those ways.

_____

_____

DAY 3

TODAY'S DIET: Hebrews 12:1; Ephesians 5:15-21
EXERCISE: Re-read the theme verse, Hebrews 12:1. Focus on the word *endurance*. According to *The New Webster's Encyclopedic Dictionary of the English Language,* the word *endurance* means "the capacity to keep going or put up with pain, hardship, etc., *for a long time.*" The survey revealed that the very thing God said is required to run the race — the lack of time — has become the number two weight hindering us as successful, victorious race runners.

• Before reading the accompanying chapters, how would you have answered this question: "Whose time is it, anyway?"

❑ God's time   ❑ my time   ❑ evil's time

• *After* reading the accompanying chapters, how do you answer that same question?

❑ God's time   ❑ my time   ❑ evil's time

• What, if any, effect does your second answer have on your own personal management of time?

_____

_____

_____

• Today's passage in Ephesians names many good things that can be done with time that has been redeemed from evil. Name some, then circle one you would like to make a priority in your life.

_____

_____

_____

DAY 4

TODAY'S DIET: Job 36:5-11

EXERCISE: God's Word is full of wise counsel that can be effectively applied to free us from the weight of the lack of time. Today's passage in Job is no exception:

(vs 5)   Who is our source of strength and understanding when it comes to effective time management?

(vs 7)   What kind of a person will receive the most help from God? How often is that help available?

(vs 8)   How does this verse describe the person with too much to do and too little time to do it?

(vs 9)   How might a person act defiantly toward God in their management of time?

(vs 10) What does God recommend as a starting point for proper time management?

(vs 11) What are the rewards of proper time management?

DAY 5

TODAY'S DIET: Mark 1:35-38

EXERCISE: In the preceding chapter, three steps were given which were necessary to anyone attempting to gain better control of their time. Those steps were:

> **Step #1:** Understand that the days are evil and that each must be redeemed.
> **Step #2:** Power up with prayer and Bible study.
> **Step #3:** Evaluate interruptions, distractions and diversions. Try to determine whether they are divine appointments or just the evil of the day surfacing.

• Today's Scripture reading recounts an interesting event, clearly illustrating how Christ demonstrated proper time management principles to those around Him.

An overriding life goal — a personal mission statement — is a must for anyone who really wants to manage their time effectively. Once that life goal is established, any and all decisions about time should fall in line with that life goal.

What was Christ's life goal according to Mark 1:38? ___

_____

How did Christ demonstrate the need of implementing Step #2? _____

What was the interruption that came? _____

_____

On the surface the interruption appeared to be a valid one for a worthy cause. Plus, the interruption came via Christ's own disciples. How did Christ implement Step #3? What role did His life goal play in His decision not to devote any additional time to the interruption? _____

_____

_____

_____

What should that tell us about implementing *all three* steps in our own lives? _____

_____

_____

22

RED AND BLACK
LETTER DAYS

I sought the Lord, and He heard me.
— Psalm 34:4

I t's amazing the number of people in the Bible who wanted to be with Jesus. Multitudes. Literally.

> Now Jesus went about all Galilee . . . and great multitudes followed Him — from Galilee, and from Decapolis, Jerusalem, Judea, and beyond the Jordan (Matt. 4:23-25).

Fishermen left their nets immediately (Matt. 4:20). Tax collectors abandoned their posts . . . one even climbed a tree just to catch a glimpse of Jesus passing by (Matt. 9:9; Luke 19:1-4). People like Nicodemus sought Him by night (John 3:1-2), and at high noon like the woman at the well (John 4:1-42).

Crowds watched for Him on the roads (Mark 10:46), waited for Him at the bottom of mountains (Matt. 17:9, 14), gathered on the shores of Galilee to hear Him teach from a boat (Matt. 13:2). They sat with Him on the hillsides for hours, forgetting about food and business and the sun setting behind them (Matt. 14:14-21).

Why? Because they wanted to be with Jesus. They wanted to spend time with Him. They wanted to talk to Him . . . tell Him their needs . . . ask Him their questions . . . feel His presence . . . listen to what He had to say. Because Jesus was different. And they felt and behaved and *were* different after they had been with Him:

> Now when they saw the boldness of Peter and John, and perceived that they were uneducated and untrained men, they marveled. And they realized that they had been with Jesus (Acts 4:13).

It shouldn't surprise us. After all, Jesus was God in the flesh. God, born in a physical body just like ours. God, walking *with* men *as* man. So when the multitudes were with Jesus, they were with *God!* And spending time with God does make a difference — in the way we feel . . . in the way we behave . . . in the way we are.

When people met Jesus, they met God in the flesh. When the leper met Jesus at the base of the mountain and begged for healing . . . when the Roman centurion came on his servant's behalf . . . when the Jewish ruler needed his daughter raised from the dead . . . it was *God* who listened.

When the disciples and the Pharisees and the rich young ruler asked Jesus questions, it was *God* in the flesh who answered.

It was interaction. It was conversation. It was *prayer!*

In our Bibles, the first four books of the New Testament are called the Gospels. There's the Gospel of Matthew, the Gospel of Mark, the Gospel of Luke, and the Gospel of John.

The word "gospel" means "good news." The Gospel of John, for instance, is the "good news" that John wrote about Jesus Christ. It's a book where John told many of the good things that he personally witnessed Jesus saying and doing.

Many New Testaments are what we call "red letter editions." That means that the text in the four Gospels is printed in alternating red and black type. As you flip through the books of Matthew, Mark, Luke, and John in a red letter edition, you see red and black . . . red and black . . . red and black.

But it's much more than just an adventure in two-color printing. It's actually a history of prayer!

The words printed in *black*, to a great extent, are the requests . . . the comments . . . the questions addressed to Jesus — God in the flesh. The words printed in black are *the prayers*. The words printed in *red* are often Jesus' answers to those prayers.

Some of the great prayers — the typical prayers — ones like ours — are found in these four books called the Gospels. And these prayers spoken to Jesus, face to face, were every bit as much prayer as other prayers recorded elsewhere in the Bible.

The plea of the leper for Jesus to heal him was just as much a prayer to God as the great intercessory prayer Moses directed heavenward in Exodus 32:31-32.

The cry of the Roman centurion for Jesus to restore his servant was just as much prayer as was Solomon's great invocation at the dedication of the completed temple (1 Kings 8:22-54). Because prayer is reaching out to God with the thoughts of our hearts . . . or the words of our lips.

The Gospels tell us that for about three years the multitudes clamored around Jesus. For three years, they spoke with Him in face-to-face prayer.

Then came Calvary — a rejected Jesus, dying on a cross outside Jerusalem. But even there, in those last hours, He answered the prayer of the desperate. God is like that. Compassionate. Listening. So when one of the two thieves crucified beside Him spoke, it was one of those red and black letter moments. We read it in the Gospel of Luke, chapter 23.

The thief prays (in a red letter edition, it's printed in black type):

> Lord, remember me when You come into Your kingdom (Luke 23:42).

Jesus answers (in red type):

> Assuredly, I say to you, today you will be with Me in Paradise (Luke 23:43).

When the thief spoke to Jesus, he realized who Jesus was — God in the flesh; and that while Jesus' body was battered and bruised . . . dying . . . the Spirit of God was present within to hear and answer his prayer.

When Jesus spoke His words of assurance, the thief didn't notice the raspy voice of a condemned and dying man. The thief heard the victorious, eternal guarantee from God of life after death in heaven forever.

Both died — the thief and Jesus. The thief went to Paradise; Jesus rose from the dead and ascended into heaven. He left behind a group of followers to carry on the work that He had begun. On their own, it would be an impossible task. Without His direction, it would fail.

The followers knew that. They still wanted to be with Jesus. They still wanted to spend time with Him. They still wanted to talk to Him . . . to tell Him their needs . . . to ask Him their questions . . . to feel His presence . . . to hear what He had to say.

That's why the first thing they did after Jesus left was pray.

> While they watched, He was taken up, and a cloud received Him out of their sight.
>
> And while they looked steadfastly toward heaven as He went up, behold, two men stood by them in white apparel, who also said, "Men of Galilee, why do you stand gazing up into heaven? This same Jesus, who was taken up from you into

heaven, will so come in like manner as you saw Him go into heaven."

Then they returned to Jerusalem. . . . And . . . they went up into the upper room where they were staying: Peter, James, John, and Andrew; Philip and Thomas; Bartholomew and Matthew; James the son of Alphaeus and Simon the Zealot; and Judas the son of James.

These all continued with one accord in prayer and supplication, with the women and Mary the mother of Jesus, and with His brothers (Acts 1:9-14).

The Book of Acts, which follows the four Gospels, records the history of Jesus' followers carrying on the job He gave them to do before He left.

Time and time again the Book of Acts mentions the prominent role that prayer played in those followers' lives:

And they continued steadfastly in the apostles' doctrine and fellowship, in the breaking of bread, and in prayers (Acts 2:42).

Now Peter and John went up together to the temple at the hour of prayer (Acts 3:1).

And when they had prayed, the place where they were assembled together was shaken; and they were all filled with the Holy Spirit, and they spoke the word of God with boldness (Acts 4:31).

We will give ourselves continually to prayer and to the ministry of the Word (Acts 6:4).

Peter went up on the housetop to pray (Acts 10:9).

Constant prayer was offered . . . by the church (Acts 12:5).

[Peter] came to the house of Mary . . . where many were gathered together praying (Acts 12:12).

When they had appointed elders in every church, and prayed with fasting, they commended them to the Lord in whom they had believed (Acts 14:23).

Now it happened, as we went to prayer (Acts 16:16).

At midnight Paul and Silas were praying and singing hymns to God, and the prisoners were listening to them (Acts 16:25).

He knelt down and prayed with them all. Then they all wept freely, and fell on Paul's neck and kissed him, sorrowing most of all for the words which he spoke, that they would see his face no more. And they accompanied him to the ship (Acts 20:36-38).

The point is, what began as face-to-face conversation between Jesus and His followers continued — and intensified — even after they could no longer see or touch Him physically. The important thing was that they could still talk to Him . . . and He could still talk to them.

But that was, as they say, "then" and this is "now." What about now? What about you?

Are you one of the modern multitudes who want to throng at the feet of Jesus? Do you long to spend time with Him? To talk to Him? To tell Him your needs . . . ask Him your questions? How long has it been since you really felt His presence . . . or heard what He had to say?

Perhaps you're like hundreds of others who need a red and black letter day — today. The good news is that it's as possible now as it was for the leper by the mountain . . . or the centurion in Capernaum . . . or for Paul and Silas in the dark jail at Philippi.

So, if you're ready, read on. If you'll supply the black letters — the prayer — He has promised to answer in red.

Let us lay aside the weight of prayerlessness . . .
and let us run with endurance
the race that is set before us.
— based on Hebrews 12:1

23

A WEIGHT INSTEAD OF WINGS

But they that wait upon the Lord
shall renew their strength;
they shall mount up with wings as eagles;
they shall run, and not be weary;
and they shall walk, and not faint.
— Isaiah 40:31;KJV

The interesting thing about the people who lived in first century Israel is how similar they were to us. It's evident when we read their conversations with Jesus that their face-to-face prayers were a lot like the prayers people pray today.

Sick people asked Jesus to heal them — if He was willing (Matt. 8:2).

People in life-threatening danger asked Jesus to save them — what's come to be known in modern war time as the "foxhole" prayer (Matt. 8:25).

Sometimes people came to Jesus to complain about others (Matt. 9:14) or to try to tell Jesus what He should do in a given situation (Matt. 14:15-19).

Other times they came asking His advice . . . or seeking an explanation of something they didn't understand (Matt. 11:2-3).

Occasionally, people worshiped Him with their words and praised Him for who He was (Matt. 16:16).

Other times they fell at His feet and reasoned with Him about why He should grant their humble requests (Matt. 15:25-28).

Sometimes people questioned Him in the same way some of us have questioned God (Matt. 15:33). Other times they made sincere promises and later discovered that promises made to God are sometimes very hard to keep (Matt. 26:35).

In each case — whether the words spoken to Jesus were words of challenge or praise or petition, He heard and answered. Sometimes it was exactly the way the pray-er hoped for; other times He answered in a way that was quite unexpected and unique.

His fame spread. Here was a Man who always listened . . . who always knew exactly what you were trying to say. Here was a Man who could answer with miracles . . . do more than you asked for . . . give you more than you had ever dreamed possible. People from all over Palestine criss-crossed the countryside to spend time with Jesus — God in the flesh — to talk with Him . . . to hear what He said in response . . . to see what He did as an answer.

Those people recognized the value of something that many of us today are letting slip away. They could have gone to the local synagogue or to the temple. They could have latched onto the nearest Pharisee. They could have grabbed a neighbor or a friend for consultation.

But they didn't. They chose to find Jesus wherever He was and talk with Him. Even when it cost time and effort.

In our survey, we asked hundreds of people to name the top three problems they felt hold us back from living a successful Christian life — from having the joy, wisdom, spiritual insight, and power God has promised His followers.

Survey respondents named many things, but prayerlessness — or the lack of personal devotions, as some called it — ranked in the top ten.

The apostle Paul wrote in our theme verse,

> Let us lay aside every weight, and run with endurance the race that is set before us (Heb. 12:1).

But as we interviewed further, we discovered that many, many of us are limping through the laps because we lack the benefits that come through prayer. Furthermore, we are carrying additional weights directly related to our personal prayerlessness.

This extra poundage includes the following:

> The weight of guilt . . . because we know that we should pray more than we do.
> Feelings of inadequacy . . . believing we don't know how to pray as we should.
> And frustration . . . because we don't know how to correct the problem.

And when we realize that what we really need to do is *pray* about our *prayerlessness*, we're really in a mess!

Especially when we realize that it was prayer — the experience itself as well as the empowerment it brings — that not only *com*pelled people to seek out Jesus wherever He was, but that also *pro*pelled the Early Church into a world-shaking posture.

How sad that now, in our time, prayer has been relegated to one of the top ten positions on a problem list for Christians! The question we need to answer is, why? Why is it so hard for us to pray? Why has prayer become a weight instead of the wings Isaiah referred to?

> But they that wait upon the Lord shall renew their strength; they shall mount up with wings as eagles; they shall run, and not be weary; and they

shall walk, and not faint (Isa. 40:31;KJV).

What did those people who spoke the words "in black" know that we do not? What was different about the multitudes who thronged around Jesus? What did they understand that we have never learned . . . or that we have forgotten? There are five things.

1. First of all, they recognized their need. They knew they needed to talk to someone with more wisdom . . . more experience . . . and more power to help.

2. They believed that Jesus could and would meet their needs — all of them.

3. They realized that time with God changes your life forever.

4. They were willing to take the time, make the sacrifice, exercise the discipline, and do whatever it took to be able to talk to . . . and hear from God.

5. They were comfortable in His presence — comfortable enough to worship Him . . . question Him . . . reason with Him . . . ask Him to intervene in impossible situations.

Keeping these five things in mind, we can effectively contrast "then" and "now." And we can discover — and correct — five reasons why prayer has become a race-losing weight instead of trophy-winning wings. So if you're ready to soar like an eagle, read on.

Let us lay aside the weight of prayerlessness . . .
and let us run with endurance
the race that is set before us.
— based on Hebrews 12:1

24

IT DOESN'T JUST HAPPEN

Thus says the Lord . . .
(the Lord of hosts is His name):
Call to Me, and I will answer you,
and show you great and mighty things,
which you do not know.
— Jeremiah 33:2-3

Physical weight gain doesn't just happen. A five pound, three ounce baby doesn't become six pounds because of some unexplainable miracle. And that extra inch around the middle that we adults often discover after holidays isn't difficult to trace. Physical weight gain is the direct result of what we eat and how much we exercise.

The same is true of spiritual weight gain. It doesn't just happen. Every problem . . . any habit . . . all the burdens that slow us down, spiritually speaking, are the direct result of our spiritual diet . . . what we believe . . . and what we say and do.

Maybe now would be a good time for you to actually pray and ask God to help you honestly evaluate your own personal prayer life and how it got to be what it is today. If the lack of prayer is one of the things that's keeping you from being the kind of Christian you really want to be, it's probably the direct result of one or more of the following five factors that contribute to our chronic prayerlessness:

1. WE DON'T TAKE PRAYER AS SERIOUSLY AS WE SHOULD.

Somewhere along the way, many of us have come to the conclusion that prayer is optional. We can choose to pray if — and when — we want to. But the truth is, prayer is not an option; it's a command:

> Everyone who is godly shall pray (Ps. 32:6).

> Take heed, watch and pray (Mark 13:33).

> Men always ought to pray and not lose heart (Luke 18:1).

> Pray without ceasing (1 Thess. 5:17).

> Pray for those who spitefully use you and persecute you (Matt. 5:44).

> Pray the Lord of the harvest to send out laborers into His harvest (Matt. 9:38).

> Is anyone among you suffering? Let him pray. . . . Is anyone among you sick? Let him call for the elders of the church, and let them pray over him, anointing him with oil in the name of the Lord. And the prayer of faith will save the sick, and the Lord will raise him up. And if he has committed sins, he will be forgiven (James 5:13-15).

> Ask, and it will be given to you; seek, and you will find; knock, and it will be opened to you (Matt. 7:7).

The Bible even goes so far as to indicate that we sin when we fail to pray for others.

Moreover, as for me, far be it from me that I should sin against the Lord in ceasing to pray for you (1 Sam. 12:23).

It is ridiculous for anyone to think they can really love or follow Jesus — really run and win the race — without spending time in prayer.

Jesus just assumed that His followers would pray. Time and time again, He gave instructions for *"when* you pray" — not, *"in case"* or *"if* you pray."

And *when you pray*, you shall not be like the hypocrites. For they love to pray standing in the synagogues and on the corners of the streets, that they may be seen by men. Assuredly, I say to you, they have their reward.

But you, *when you pray*, go into your room, and when you have shut your door, pray to your Father who is in the secret place; and your Father who sees in secret will reward you openly.

But *when you pray*, do not use vain repetitions as the heathen do. For they think that they will be heard for their many words (Matt. 6:5-7).

Therefore I say to you, whatever things you ask *when you pray*, believe that you receive them, and you will have them (Mark 11:24).

When you pray, say: Our Father in heaven, hallowed be Your name. Your kingdom come. Your will be done On earth as it is in heaven (Luke 11:2).

Losing the weight of prayerlessness is like any other weight loss or weight management program. It requires that we first take it seriously. And when we begin to see that prayer is a serious matter — and that prayerlessness is a very serious condition — we are on our way to running the race a little lighter.

But there's a second reason prayer has become a weight instead of wings in America today:

2. WE'VE NEVER MADE PRAYER A HABIT — EXCEPT, PERHAPS, AT MEALTIMES.

If prayer at mealtimes is a habit, good for you! But think about the way it became a habit. It's because you implemented a two-step program: First of all, you decided to pray at a specific time (mealtime); and secondly, you do it each time *that time* rolls around. Habits are formed over time.

Even Jesus practiced praying at mealtimes:

> And when He had taken the five loaves and the two fish, He looked up to heaven, blessed and broke the loaves, and gave them to His disciples (Mark 6:41).

> And He commanded the multitude to sit down on the ground. And He took the seven loaves and gave thanks, broke them and gave them to His disciples to set before them; and they set them before the multitude (Mark 8:6).

> And He took bread, gave thanks and broke it, and gave it to them (Luke 22:19).

But obviously, even habitual prayer to thank God for food at mealtimes is not enough to give us wings to soar and strength to run, unwearied. Which brings us to a third reason why we don't pray as we should.

3. WE'VE EXCHANGED OUR SENSE OF NEED FOR PRIDE IN OUR OWN SELF-SUFFICIENCY.

Most of us are blessed beyond measure — to the point of a curse. When we need food, we go to the grocery store and buy it. Each month, there's money in the bank to write a check for rent or a house payment. Our jobs come with excellent benefits including health care and dental coverage.

If we're contemplating a business deal, experts are at our fingertips by phone, fax, or e-mail, over lunch or via corporate meeting in the boardroom. If we're mad at our spouse . . . enraged with a friend . . . ready to sue a total stranger . . . we have confidants and counselors and legal advice available in abundance.

We're just about as self-sufficient as anyone in the world has ever been. In fact, we've become so self-sufficient that even the few prayers we do pray have changed.

It used to be that most of our prayers were nothing but "Gimme" prayers — prayers with little praise and even less intercession for others. But now we've taken such pride in our own ability to network and provide for ourselves, that even the Gimme prayers are few and far between.

So much so, in fact, that what the apostle John wrote in Revelation 3:17-20 seems to fit us:

> Because you say, "I am rich, have become wealthy, and have need of nothing" — and do not know that you are wretched, miserable, poor, blind, and naked — I counsel you to buy from Me gold refined in the fire, that you may be rich; and white garments, that you may be clothed, that the shame of your nakedness may not be revealed; and anoint your eyes with eye salve, that you may see. As many as I love, I rebuke and chasten. Therefore be zealous and repent. Behold, I stand at the door and knock. If anyone hears My voice and opens the door, I will come in to him and dine with him, and he with Me.

Interesting, isn't it, that the last sentence in that passage describes what the people who talked face-to-face with Jesus experienced — fellowship . . . camaraderie . . . interaction . . . communication . . . conversation . . . time with God!

Oddly enough, some of us avoid that kind of time with God — the kind of time we experience in prayer — because . . .

4. WE'RE NOT COMFORTABLE IN GOD'S PRESENCE.

We don't know what He looks like, so it's hard to picture Him. We worry about getting in the proper mood . . . about what we should say first and middle and last . . . if we should pray out loud or if we can just "think" our prayers to heaven.

We try different positions . . . pray in various places . . . copy the prayers of others who seem to pray the "right" kind of prayers.

Although the Bible encourages us to "come boldly to the throne of grace" in prayer (Heb. 4:16), most of the time, we approach timidly . . . feeling inadequate . . . unsure and uncomfortable.

It helps when we remember that even the apostle Paul admitted that *he* didn't know how to pray as he should. So, if you feel that *you* don't know how to pray — you're in quality company!

The thing that Paul did, however, was pray anyway, realizing that the Holy Spirit helps us to pray as we should. The Holy Spirit takes over where our own feeble attempts at prayer leave off:

> Likewise the Spirit also helps in our weaknesses. For we do not know what we should pray for as we ought, but the Spirit Himself makes intercession for us with groanings which cannot be uttered (Rom. 8:26).

It also helps to remember that there are many things we don't automatically know how to do. We weren't born knowing how to drive a car, for instance; but when we see the need and the value of it, we learn and practice every day.

The same principle applies to prayer. We may not have been born knowing how to pray, but when we realize our need of prayer, and the value of prayer, we should be challenged to begin to learn and practice it every day.

Remember that Peter requested that Jesus teach the disciples *"to* pray," not *"how* to pray." There is no set format . . . no specific time of day that's best . . . no special words to say . . . no position or place that's more proper than others.

Just as your conversation varies with friends and family each time you see them, so your conversation with your Best Friend will vary.

A review of the red and black "prayers" of the Gospels will soon convince you that there is no set way in which you must pray. Those first followers of Jesus prayed standing . . . sitting . . . kneeling. They prayed loudly . . . in their thoughts . . . on the water . . . even while being crucified. They prayed at various times about various things.

But no matter how they prayed, Jesus understood. And when we pray — no matter how well or how imperfectly, He still hears and understands — plus, the Holy Spirit takes over, making up for our inadequacies!

So, what other possible reasons could there be for not praying? Perhaps . . .

5. WE'RE AFRAID THAT IF WE PRAYED, GOD MIGHT ANSWER.

There's an interesting verse found in Mark 9:32. In verse 31, Jesus told the disciples that He was going to be killed and that He would rise from the dead the third day. Then, verse 32:

> But [the disciples] did not understand this saying, and were afraid to ask Him.

Sometimes we're afraid of what God seems to be saying or doing in our lives. And we're equally afraid to go to

Him in prayer and ask. We're afraid that He might answer with something we don't want to hear or experience . . . something that doesn't quite fit our agenda . . . something we would really rather not go through.

Acts 13:2 tells us about what happened one time when the Christians in Antioch prayed:

> As they ministered to the Lord and fasted, the Holy Spirit said, "Now separate to Me Barnabas and Saul for the work to which I have called them."

Many of us are afraid that if we pray, God will ask *us* to separate from some things. We might have to change our plans . . . re-evaluate our desires . . . give up some time . . . part with some money . . . move out of our comfort zone.

So we avoid the risk. (And risk more than we ever dreamed possible.) We exchange prayer for prayerlessness, and we wind up with an unbearable weight instead of wings.

SO WHAT'S THE SOLUTION?

If you're 10 pounds overweight, you don't generally lose all 10 pounds instantaneously. But if you don't start trying, you won't lose any. And if you don't discipline yourself to keep at it, you'll never be completely rid of it.

The same is true with the weight of prayerlessness. To begin losing it, try this three-step plan:

1. Decide how much "weight" you need to lose. Re-think the five previous reasons that can cause prayerlessness. Do any seem to be true in your life? If so, how many of them? And which ones?
2. Begin praying. Start today.
3. Keep at it. Make prayer a habit.

Begin in obedience. Continue as discipline. You'll quickly discover the sheer delight as well as the multiple rewards that come as a result of talking and listening to God.

Before long, you'll find yourself looking forward to spending time with Jesus. You'll seek Him out as the multitudes — the "people in black" — did so very long ago. You'll be experiencing your own personal red and black letter days.

Let us lay aside the weight of prayerlessness . . .
and let us run with endurance
the race that is set before us.
— based on Hebrews 12:1

PART 8
LET US LAY ASIDE THE WEIGHT OF
PRAYERLESSNESS

In a recent survey, hundreds of people were asked to name the top three "weights" they felt were facing Christians in America today. One of the top ten was *prayerlessness* — a stark contrast to the days when the crowds clamored to talk and listen to Jesus.

This week, determine if and how much of a weight of prayerlessness you are carrying. Each day, focus on one of the five main reasons why the area of prayer can become "weight" instead of wings.

DAY 1

REASON 1: We don't take prayer as seriously as we should.
TODAY'S DIET: Psalm 32:1-6
EXERCISE: Honestly assess how you feel about prayer. Complete this sentence:

> I believe prayer is:
> ❏ an option for a believer.
> ❏ an obligation for every believer.

Now assess, not how you *feel,* but how you *operate:*

> I act as though I believe prayer is:
> ❏ an option for a believer.
> ❏ an obligation for every believer.

• Jesus said, "If you love Me, keep my commandments." And *prayer* is a commandment! To help you take prayer more seriously than you already do, select several of the following verses to meditate upon:

Matthew 5:44	Matthew 9:38	Matthew 26:41
Mark 13:33	Luke 18:1	James 5:13
Matthew 7:7	1 Timothy 2:1	1 Peter 4:7
Ephesians 6:17-18		

• It is ridiculous for anyone to think they can really love or follow Jesus — really run and win the race — without spending time in prayer. Jesus *assumed* His followers would pray. Look up the following verses in your Bible and underline the words "*when* you pray" in each of them:

Then, write in the space provided below what we are to do "when we pray."

Matthew 6:5 _____

Matthew 6:6 _____

Matthew 6:7 _____

Mark 11:24 _____

DAY 2

REASON 2: We've never made prayer a habit — except at meal-times.

TODAY'S DIET: Luke 11:1-13

EXERCISE: Do you usually pray at mealtimes? At bedtime? If so, you have formed a habit. How was that habit formed? _____

_____

_____

• Read Daniel 6:10. What does this verse say about Daniel's prayer habit? _____

_____

_____

• Read *Luke 4:16.* What habit did Jesus have? _____

_____

_____

• Read the following verses. What do they tell you about Jesus' prayer habits?

• Mark 6:46 _____

• Luke 6:11 _____

• Luke 6:12 _____

• Luke 9:28-29 _____

• Luke 11:1 _____

DAY 3

REASON 3: We've exchanged our sense of need for a sense of pride in our own self-sufficiency
TODAY'S DIET: Revelation 3:17-21
EXERCISE: Which of the following things do you regularly ask the Lord to provide?

    ❑ food   ❑ clothing
    ❑ shelter   ❑ health/health care

• Which of the following do you more or less feel you provide for yourself?

    ❑ food   ❑ clothing
    ❑ shelter   ❑ health/health care

• Which of the following do you regularly thank the Lord for?

    ❑ food   ❑ clothing
    ❑ shelter   ❑ health/health care

• The number one sin in God's eyes is pride. The number one virtue is humility. We express pride when we harbor an attitude of self-sufficiency. We manifest humility when we depend on Him. Dependence is an outgrowth of humility.

Read Matthew 6:33 and memorize it if you have not already.

DAY 4

REASON 4: We're not comfortable in His presence; we think we don't know the proper format for prayer.
TODAY'S DIET: Romans 8:26-39
EXERCISE: If Scripture is clear about anything, it is that

there is no prescribed format for prayer. People are recorded praying in a variety of positions . . . while in numerous kinds of locations . . . at different times of the day and night . . . about various things.

Look up the following verses. Draw lines to match each reference with the variable it contains.

- standing
- kneeling
- lying prostrate
- walking on water
- sitting down
- hanging on cross
- in bed
- in times of trouble
- before meals
- in a solitary place
- with others
- at evening, morning, and noon

- 1 Kings 18:42
- Matthew 14:23
- Psalm 50:15
- Luke 18:13
- Matthew 18:19-20
- Luke 23:42
- Psalm 55:16-17
- Luke 22:41
- Matthew 26:39
- Psalm 63:6
- Matthew 14:30
- Matthew 14:19

DAY 5

REASON 5: We're afraid that if we pray, God might answer.

TODAY'S DIET: Mark 9:30-32; Acts 13:1-3

EXERCISE: In the Mark 9 passage, the disciples did not understand something, and were afraid to ask the Lord about it. Is there something you are currently having trouble understanding? If so, what? _____

_____

_____

• Sometimes we're afraid to pray because we're afraid God might answer and ask us to change or adjust some things in our lives. In the Acts 13 passage, the church prayed and the Lord asked them to give up two of their finest leaders. Which of the following things would *you* be willing to give up if the Lord asked you to do so in response to *your* prayers?

❑ plans ❑ desires ❑ time
❑ money ❑ position ❑ comfort zone

• If prayerlessness has become a weight in your life, take steps TODAY to correct it. Prayerlessness is a serious matter. If you are not craving time alone with the Lord, consider it a warning. Matthew 5:6 says, "Blessed are those who hunger and thirst after righteousness, For they shall be filled." If you are not hungering and thirsting, begin these steps toward *prayerfulness* today!

1. Decide how much "weight" you need to lose. Re-think the five previous reasons that can cause prayerlessness. Do any seem to be true in your life? If so, how many of them? And which ones?
2. Begin praying. Start today.
3. Keep at it. Make prayer a habit. Begin in obedience. Continue as discipline.

• Begin a daily or weekly prayer journal, noting the things you have prayed about, the answers you have received, and the impressions you believe came from the Lord as you spent time with Him.

25

FORMALLY FORGIVEN

Fervent lips with a wicked heart
are like earthenware covered with silver dross.
He who hates, disguises it with his lips,
and lays up deceit within himself;
when he speaks kindly, do not believe him,
for there are seven abominations in his heart.
— Proverbs 26:23-25

The year 1974 was momentous in our nation's history. May 9 impeachment hearings against our president were opened by the House Judiciary Committee. Exactly three months later, on August 9, at 12:00 noon, Richard Milhous Nixon, the 37th president of the United States, resigned.

But just one month later, on September 8, President Gerald R. Ford granted an "absolute unconditional" pardon to ex-President Nixon for all federal crimes that he "committed or may have committed" while president.

That presidential pardon, signed on behalf of the nation, was a formal release. It meant that no related charges could ever be filed against former President Nixon. He was excused . . . ceremonially absolved . . . officially forgiven.

But only officially. Because in reality, as a nation, we

never really forgave him. Other nations did. In fact, they even welcomed Richard Nixon as a respected statesman. But not us.

The "Nixon Era" and "Watergate" are still referred to as America's dark days. Commentators still use Richard Nixon as the one good example of what *not* to do or be as president. And many people felt until the day he died, that "Tricky Dick" never really got was what coming to him.

Our resentment has been a weight we've carried as a nation through every subsequent political election. Like a dead fish, it's floated to the top of every political scandal since. It's a heavy, hardened attitude that surfaces every time we hear his name, or spot corruption in high places.

That's the way it often is with our so-called "forgiveness."

Someone wrongs us — a friend or a co-worker who said something unkind . . . a spouse or a parent who mistreated you. The boss who fired you . . . a child who hurt you . . . a relative who disgraced you.

They wrong us, then ask for forgiveness; and most of us are big enough to issue an "official pardon." We say the right words — maybe even pray together. But deep down, we harbor resentment. And the mere mention of that person's name dredges up all kinds of bad memories and even worse feelings.

We bring up that person — or that hurtful event — in our conversations with others for years to come. Forever after, we approach everything the offender says or does with suspicion. We avoid them in person and hesitate to return their calls. And if by chance we hear that something unfortunate has happened to them, we silently rejoice, because all the time "they had it coming to them" anyway.

We might call it the Nixon/Ford Forgiveness Syndrome. Or "going through the formality of forgiveness."

But the truth is, words of forgiveness are empty and meaningless unless you have the solid gold bars of *true* forgiveness on deposit in your heart's inner vault.

Without that collateral, the words "I forgive you" are nothing more than cheap imitations of the real thing. Like a silver-coated clay pitcher pretending to be a fine silver teapot. Earthenware covered with dross, the Bible calls it.

Like President Ford's pardon of Richard Nixon, you can go through the formality of forgiveness and it's "official." But deep down, the hard feelings can linger, and you and God both know they're there.

But maybe what you don't know is how many other people there are — good people — who are just like you. Like you, they've been wronged. Hurt. Stepped on.

Many of them have even tried their best to forgive, just like you. They've said the words, sent the flowers, and delivered the candy. But they have never really been able to forgive.

Hundreds of them responded to the weight loss survey, admitting that of all the things holding them back — slowing them down — keeping them from being the kind of a person we all want to be — "unforgiveness" ranked sixth in a list of the top ten.

That means that many of us — sinners, one and all — Christians, who have experienced the absolute, unconditional pardon of God — are still having problems extending the same grace of forgiveness to others who have wronged us.

Do you remember what the apostle Paul told Timothy about unforgiveness? He linked it with "the last days" — the days just prior to the second coming of Jesus Christ. Paul wrote,

> But know this, that in the last days perilous times will come: For men will be lovers of themselves . . . proud . . . unloving, unforgiving . . . headstrong . . . having a form of godliness but denying its power (2 Tim. 3:1-5).

That pretty much describes the kind of a world we're living in right now, doesn't it? Chances are you've run into at least one of these headstrong, unloving, unforgiving characters in the recent past. But the chances are also good that a little of that same proud, headstrong attitude so prevalent in our world today has also rubbed off on you.

Perhaps you are one of hundreds bogged down in the race of life by the excess weight of unforgiveness. Perhaps right now, you're remembering someone that you've never really forgiven.

Maybe you need to forgive yourself. Maybe you've been blaming God for something and need to forgive Him. Maybe it's the person who used to be your closest friend. Maybe it's someone you hardly knew or never knew at all.

Perhaps you don't really think forgiveness is all that important. Or maybe you don't really want to forgive. But perhaps you should consider this before you make your final decision:

Forgiveness is a gift you give yourself.

That gift has already been paid for. It's been in layaway — perhaps for a long, long while. So . . . isn't it time you thought about picking it up and opening it?

Let us lay aside the weight of unforgiveness . . .
and let us run with endurance
the race that is set before us.
— based on Hebrews 12:1

26

SOMETHING FISHY ABOUT UNFORGIVENESS

This is an evil generation.
It seeks a sign, and no sign will be given to it
except the sign of Jonah the prophet.
— Luke 11:29

For some reason, when we think of forgiveness, we think of the benefits the *other* person receives who is forgiven. Sometimes just the thought that a wrong-doer could actually profit from our forgiveness hinders any desire on our part to forgive.

We don't want them to feel better or be better off because we have forgiven them. We want them to suffer. They did wrong and they should have to pay for it.

Jonah felt that way.

You remember Jonah — from "Jonah and the Whale." It was probably one of the first Bible stories you ever heard.

One day, God told Jonah to go to the city of Nineveh. God wanted Jonah to tell the people of Nineveh that God loved them and wanted to forgive them of their sin.

Jonah, however, caught a boat and went in the opposite direction; so God sent a terrible storm at sea. Jonah told the sailors that God was angry with him, and that the only way to stop the storm was by throwing him overboard. After all other attempts to save the ship failed, they did.

Meanwhile, God had prepared a great fish to swallow Jonah. Jonah spent three miserable days and three miserable nights in the belly of the fish. He had a lot of time to think about his attitude. Finally, Jonah asked God to forgive him. God spoke to the fish and it threw up — Jonah and all — on the dry land.

Many people, after hearing the story of Jonah, conclude that disobedience was Jonah's main problem . . . that the reason God sent the storm and allowed Jonah to do hard time in a slippery belly was because he disobeyed God and went in the opposite direction from Nineveh.

But the truth is, Jonah's main problem was *unforgiveness*. It was unforgiveness that led both to his disobedience — and his distasteful trip backwards through the digestive tract of a great big fish!

And by the way, if you're carrying a similar weight of unforgiveness, you are already sinking as low as Jonah did — without the protection of a God-prepared fish to surround and protect you!

But let's look at, as Paul Harvey would say, the rest of the story. God had told Jonah to go to Nineveh. But Nineveh was the capital of the most cruel conquering empire in the ancient world — Assyria.

Jonah knew all about the Assyrians. They had raided and ravaged his homeland and tortured his countrymen. Some of them had their tongues ripped out by the roots. Others were skinned alive; their skins hung on the defeated cities' walls. Many were killed outright and their decapitated heads stacked to form decorative pyramids along the conquered roadways of Israel. The Assyrians had burned the children alive, taken the women into slavery, and completely destroyed the cities and surrounding farmland.

Now, into this new picture of Nineveh, position Jonah. Jonah, the preacher that God wanted to use to tell the Assyrians about His love. Jonah, the man like us who couldn't find it in himself to forgive . . . to share the message of redemption . . . to go with good news into the enemy's camp.

Jonah wanted the Assyrians to suffer for what they had done. He wanted them to die, never hearing about God's offer of salvation. Jonah wanted them to spend eternity in hell. They deserved it. (But so did he. And so do we.)

Jonah, weighted down with unforgiveness, sank to the bottom of the deep blue sea in the belly of a great big fish.

Now you would think that after all Jonah went through in that fish, that he could have forgiven just about anyone for anything. But he couldn't . . . and didn't.

When God asked Jonah the second time to go and preach to the Assyrians, Jonah did, in fact, go. Nineveh had walls 100 feet high and wide enough for three chariots to travel on side by side. It took three days to travel from one end of Nineveh to the other.

But when Jonah preached, the capital city was rocked. Revival broke out. The king proclaimed a fast — nothing to eat or drink. Everyone — man and beast — was commanded to put on rough sackcloth, and every citizen was ordered to cry out to God for mercy.

The people of Nineveh were genuinely sorry for the evil they had done. And God forgave them. But Jonah did not.

Jonah also cried out to God — in anger. "See Lord, I knew You'd do this," Jonah said. "That's why I headed for Tarshish in the first place. I *knew* You wouldn't punish them. That's just the way You are. Why, You'd forgive *anybody* no matter what they've done!" (Jonah 4:1-2).

The last picture we have of Jonah, he is sitting under a wilted plant . . . the hot sun beating down on him. He's wishing to die . . . sinking even lower under the weight of unforgiveness than he had been before in the belly of the fish. Even worse, as the picture fades, Jonah is totally out of fellowship with God — the One who had spoken to the fish and delivered him before.

To our knowledge, Jonah never experienced what others have learned: that forgiveness is a gift we give ourselves.

And like the floral commercial says, "It's the gift that keeps on giving." Once you start opening it, you'll find lots of other gifts nested together inside.

So perhaps we should really say, Forgiveness is the *gifts* you give yourself. Let's start unwrapping them.

FORGIVENESS IS A GIFT YOU GIVE YOURSELF BECAUSE IT BRINGS THE REWARDS OF OBEDIENCE.

In Galatians 5:22-23, we're given a list of qualities that are called "the fruit of the Spirit." The nine assets that are listed are love, joy, peace, long-suffering, kindness, goodness, faithfulness, gentleness, and self-control. Forgiveness is noticeably missing.

While forgiveness itself is not a fruit of the Spirit, it is totally dependent on the operation of the fruit of the Spirit in our lives. Because without that fruit — without that help from the Holy Spirit — we wind up with a mere guise of godliness and no power to forgive.

Furthermore, *un*forgiveness is the *opposite* of the fruit of the Spirit because it is completely contrary to the nature of love, joy, peace, long-suffering, kindness, goodness, faithfulness, gentleness, and self-control.

Forgiveness is not a fruit of the Spirit; forgiveness is a command that must be obeyed by an act of the will . . . by dying to self and subordinating our natural tendencies and desires to vindicate ourselves.

> You shall not hate your brother in your heart. . . . You shall not take vengeance, nor bear any grudge against the children of your people, but you shall love your neighbor as

yourself: I am the Lord (Lev. 19:17-18).

Because we are commanded to forgive, each time when we obey that command and forgive someone who has wronged us, we place ourselves in a position where God can bless us; He can reward us for our obedience to His Word:

He who despises the word will be destroyed, but he who fears the commandment will be rewarded (Prov. 13:13).

If you are willing and obedient, you shall eat the good of the land (Isa. 1:19).

Obey My voice, and I will be your God, and you shall be My people. And walk in all the ways that I have commanded you, that it may be well with you (Jer. 7:23).

Whoever hears these sayings of Mine, and does them, I will liken him to a wise man who built his house on the rock: and the rain descended, the floods came, and the winds blew and beat on that house; and it did not fall, for it was founded on the rock (Matt. 7:24-25).

Blessed are those who hear the word of God and keep it! (Luke 11:28).

If you keep My commandments, you will abide in My love (John 15:10).

Behold, I set before you today a blessing and a curse: the blessing, if you obey the commandments of the Lord your God which I command you today; and the curse, if you do not obey the commandments of the Lord your God (Deut. 11:26-28).

FORGIVENESS IS A GIFT YOU GIVE YOURSELF BECAUSE IT WILL MAKE YOU MORE GOD-LIKE AND MORE CHRIST-LIKE.

When we are ready to forgive rather than blame . . . to forget rather than resent, we are becoming more like our Heavenly Father and His Son, the Lord Jesus Christ.

Paul wrote,

> And be kind to one another, tenderhearted, forgiving one another, just as God in Christ also forgave you" (Eph. 4:32).

And the Psalmist said,

> For You, Lord, are good, and ready to forgive, And abundant in mercy to all those who call upon You (Ps. 86:5).

As we become more like God, we are fulfilling God's purpose for our lives. Romans 8:28 is a favorite verse to claim when "bad" things happen to us. We comfort ourselves with the knowledge that when it comes to His children, God uses events and circumstances, that appear "bad" to us, in order to bring about good.

But the following verse, verse 29, tells us what at least a part of that "good" is:

> And we know that all things work together for good to those who love God, to those who are the called according to His purpose. For whom He foreknew, He also pre-destined to be conformed to the image of His Son, that He might be the firstborn among many brethren (Rom. 8:28-29).

When someone wrongs us, it's hard to think of it as anything but "bad." But Romans 8:28-29 tells us that God can use that event — from a single rude comment to a lifetime of abuse — to bring about good in our lives. And a part of that "good" is being conformed to — or molded in — the image of Jesus.

What was Jesus like? Compassionate. Forgiving. Even of those who rejected and crucified Him. From the cross, some of Jesus' last words were,

> Father, forgive them, for they do not know what they do (Luke 23:34).

Is it possible that God has given you the opportunity to become more Christ-like by allowing someone to wrong you — someone He wants you to forgive?

FORGIVENESS IS A GIFT YOU GIVE YOURSELF BECAUSE IT WILL MAKE YOU A MORE EFFECTIVE WITNESS.

Forgiveness puts your money where your mouth is. The apostle Paul wrote the church at Corinth and said in effect,

> What are you guys thinking? You're going to court — believer against believer! And you're doing it in front of unbelievers! How can you possibly tell others that *they* need to get right with God when you can't even settle a small matter among yourselves? You ought to be ashamed! Forgive and forget. Try to save what little witness you have left! (1 Cor. 6:1-8; paraphrased).

Unforgiveness and its accompanying poundage — resentment . . . bitterness . . . malice . . . revenge — will kill any testimony you have. It's impossible to talk to others about what God's forgiveness and the change it makes in our lives if we, ourselves, cannot forgive.

Having the desire — and demonstrating the ability — to genuinely forgive is what makes what we say about God more convincing than what the rest of the world says about Him. Without the ability to forgive, we are little more than what the world thinks of us anyway — that we are nothing but mouthy hypocrites.

Forgiveness is the quality that makes what you say about being a Christian uniquely different . . . powerful . . . and best of all, believable.

FORGIVENESS IS A GIFT YOU GIVE YOURSELF BECAUSE IT MAKES LIFE MORE ENJOYABLE.

Forgiving will help solve every problem that will ever come in any relationship you will ever have. Forgiveness relieves stress and tension, builds and maintains relationships, and helps make work, your home, even church a harmonious and fun place to be and serve.

The Psalmist wrote,

> Behold, how good and how pleasant it is For brethren to dwell together in unity! (Ps. 133:1).

The benefits of forgiveness obviously enhance emotional and mental and spiritual health, but they often extend to physical well-being as well.

I remember just such an example that I personally witnessed. A woman had traveled across the state and asked to see me. I agreed to counsel her, because we shared a mutual friend. I noticed what a toll arthritis had taken on the burdened woman.

The woman began pouring out her heart — how she had been wronged by a family member. It was a sad story, and it was clear that she had been genuinely mistreated. But it also became clear that the real thing crippling her was not arthritis, but being unable to forgive.

I began sharing the benefits of forgiveness. The woman listened carefully and seemed to agree; so I attempted to lead her in a prayer of forgiveness.

"Just repeat these words after me," I said. "Dear God, I forgive _____," and I named the person who had wronged her.

But the woman bolted. She couldn't do it.

I counseled further, and tried to lead her in prayer again. Five or six times, I tried — but with the same results each time. Her unforgiveness had driven long roots of bitterness deep into every area of her life.

At long last, she choked out the prayer, and left.

A couple of hours later, the phone rang. It was the woman.

"Pastor," she said, "I'm at a pay telephone. I couldn't wait until I got home. I've been doing what you told me to do in the car. I've been thanking God — out loud — that I was able to forgive _____. I even asked God to bless her!

"And guess what happened?! I had my hands on the steering wheel and all of the knots disappeared! Pastor, I tell you the truth — even that knot on my back is gone! I feel so free! I just had to stop and call!"

If you have a chronic illness, it wouldn't hurt to do a fast forgiveness check-up — just in case!

FORGIVENESS IS A GIFT YOU GIVE YOURSELF BECAUSE IT FORESTALLS FURTHER, MORE SERIOUS PROBLEMS.

We've already seen the classic example — Jonah. Unforgiveness led to disobedience and rebellion. Disobedience and rebellion led to problems for innocent bystanders — the sailors. Because of Jonah, they were forced to dump their cargo in the sea and eventually, to throw Jonah overboard, as well.

Sure, Jonah repented, and his repentance even led to a revival; but Jonah had never really conquered his unforgiving spirit. So when the Ninevites repented and God forgave them, Jonah's unforgiveness sprouted again because the root of bitterness toward the Assyrians had never been fully uprooted.

Unforgiveness will cause the same kinds of problems

in your life. You'll have problems in relationships — even with total strangers. It will stir up storms and whale-sized predicaments that will swallow you up and spit you out on foreign territory.

And the problems are guaranteed to grow progressively worse — until you either deal with the underlying cause of unforgiveness, or disappear into obscurity as Jonah did.

The Bible says,

> Pursue peace with all men, and holiness, without which no one will see the Lord: looking diligently lest anyone fall short of the grace of God; lest any root of bitterness springing up cause trouble, and by this many become defiled (Heb. 12:14-15).

If these benefits are not enough to encourage you to foster a forgiving spirit, turn the page. Because the advantages of forgiving others — even your worst enemies — gets even better yet!

Let us lay aside the weight of unforgiveness . . .
and let us run with endurance
the race that is set before us.
— based on Hebrews 12:1

27

THOSE WHO ARE DEAD AGAINST US

When a man's ways please the Lord,
He makes even his enemies to be at peace with him.
— Proverbs 16:7

When it comes to a proper attitude about forgiveness, a little boy saying his bedtime prayers got it right:

> Our Father, which art in heaven,
> Hallowed be Thy name.
> Thy kingdom come.
> Thy will be done in earth, as it is in heaven.
> Give us this day our daily bread.
> And forgive us our debts
> as we forgive those who are dead against us. . . .

That's a difficult task — forgiving someone who is dead against you. Just ask Jonah. But when you forgive, it catches the attention of God, and it's as if He says, "Grab the scissors and cut the ribbon," because forgiveness is the gift that truly keeps on giving!

FORGIVENESS IS A GIFT YOU GIVE YOURSELF BECAUSE IT FREES GOD TO WORK ON YOUR BEHALF AGAINST YOUR OPPOSITION.

This is one of the great mysteries of God, so read it again: Forgiveness frees God to work on your behalf *against your opposition.* He's better equipped to handle the opposition than you are, anyway!

Take a moment and do this exercise: Think about someone who wronged you . . . someone who *really wronged* you. No two ways about it — even *God* knows that they were wrong and you were right.

Now here's the acid test of true and total forgiveness. Consider how you would feel if you heard that something bad had happened to that person. Would you feel even a little bit glad way deep down inside? Because if you would, you haven't really forgiven them.

Proverbs 17:5 says,

> He who is glad at calamity will not go unpunished.

And Proverbs 24:17-18 says,

> Do not rejoice when your enemy falls, and
> do not let your heart be glad when he stumbles;
> lest the Lord see it, and it displease Him, and He
> turn away His wrath from him.

Did you notice that last phrase — *"lest the Lord see it* [your unforgiveness], *and it displease Him, and He turn away His wrath from him* [the person who wronged you]."

It is only when we release all of our unforgiveness and all our desire for vengeance that God steps in to work on our behalf against those who have wronged us. And the moment we pick up that weight of unforgiveness again, God withdraws and withholds His intervening hand.

Bless those who persecute you; bless and do not curse (Rom. 12:14).

Beloved, do not avenge yourselves, but rather give place to wrath for it is written, "Vengeance is Mine, I will repay," says the Lord. Therefore if your enemy hungers, feed him; if he thirsts, give him a drink; for in so doing you will heap coals of fire on his head (Rom. 12:19-20).

That means give up your *own* wrath to allow God's righteous, perfect wrath to handle the situation as He sees fit — for His glory and for *your* good.

Forgiveness is a gift we give ourselves because it frees God to work against our opposition, and . . .

FORGIVENESS IS A GIFT YOU GIVE YOURSELF BECAUSE IT FREES GOD TO WORK ON YOUR BEHALF TO BLESS YOU.

The Bible tells us about the man, Job, who had lost his wealth, his health, and his children. His wife scoffed at him and his faith. His three friends came to comfort him, but wound up condemning him.

Job forgave them. And more than that, he heaped coals of fire on their heads. He prayed for them. And it freed God to bless him:

And the Lord restored Job's losses when he prayed for his friends.

Indeed the Lord gave Job twice as much as he had before. Then all his brothers, all his sisters, and all those who had been his acquaintances before, came to him and ate food with him in his house; and they consoled him and comforted him for all the adversity that the Lord had brought upon him. Each one gave him a piece of silver and each a ring of gold.

Now the Lord blessed the latter days of Job more than his beginning (Job 42:10-12).

And finally,

FORGIVENESS IS A GIFT YOU GIVE YOURSELF BECAUSE BY FORGIVING, YOU SOW SEEDS OF FORGIVENESS THAT YOU WILL REAP FROM OTHERS LATER ON.

In His model prayer, Jesus said,

And forgive us our debts, As we forgive our debtors" (Matt. 6:12).

And then the Master said,

For if you forgive men their trespasses [offenses], your heavenly Father will also forgive you (Matt. 6:14).

Judge not, and you shall not be judged. Condemn not, and you shall not be condemned. Forgive, and you will be forgiven (Luke 6:37).

And Paul summed it up by telling the believers at Galatia,

Do not be deceived, God is not mocked; for whatever a man sows, that he will also reap. . . . And let us not grow weary while doing good, for in due season we shall reap if we do not lose heart. Therefore, as we have opportunity, let us do good to all, especially to those who are of the household of faith (Gal. 6:7-10).

The FTD commercials say, "Give the gift that keeps on giving." And that's what forgiveness is . . . the gift you give yourself that keeps on giving. The challenge, then, for us is to take four bold steps toward losing the weight of unforgiveness:

1. Step on honest scales (Prov. 11:1; 20:10).

Are you carrying a weight of unforgiveness?

Walk through the chambers of your heart to the very darkest back room. Look at the dart board hanging on the wall. Is there a picture of someone in the middle? Someone you haven't ever been able to really forgive? If there is . . .

2. Ask yourself, What did that person do or say to wrong me?

Was there any validity — any truth to what they said?

Was there any reason — something I did or said to cause them to do what they did?

If so . . .

3. Confess any wrong-doing on *your* part to the Lord right now.

And remember to confess all the resentment . . . malice . . . unforgiveness you've been feeling. Then, take a deep breath and . . .

4. If at all possible, make it right with the other person involved.

Forgiveness begins with an official pardon, and is followed by the right attitude; but it's sealed with action.

Inward attitude and outward speech are just the down payment on real forgiveness. It takes regular installments of kind deeds and thoughts to mark the mortgage paid in full.

Peter asked,

> "Lord, how often shall my brother sin against me, and I forgive him? Up to seven times?"
> Jesus said to him, "I do not say to you, up to seven times, but up to seventy times seven" (Matt. 18:21-22).

We probably make a mistake if we assume that Jesus meant that if someone *sins against us 490 times*, we are to forgive them each time. It is more likely that Jesus was saying that we may have to consciously forgive the *same* person for the *same thing* 490 times before we *really* have forgiven them to the point that we can feed them . . . give them a drink . . . pray for them as Job did . . . rejoice when God blesses them as He blessed the Ninevites.

God, in His infinite wisdom, knows us very well. He understands the kind of weight that unforgiveness can become. He knows that when we are hurt, that hurt lingers in our subconscious, ready to surface day by day, time after time.

That's why each time the hurt . . . or the wrong-doer comes to mind, Jesus said, "Forgive." Make a conscious effort to say, "I have forgiven . . . I have forgiven . . . I have forgiven . . . 410 times . . . 420 times . . . 450 times . . . 475 . . . 489 . . . 490.

Then step on the scales. You'll discover the dead weight of unforgiveness is gone; and you're running the race as you've never run before.

Let us lay aside the weight of unforgiveness . . .
and let us run with endurance
the race that is set before us.
— based on Hebrews 12:1

PART 9
LET US LAY ASIDE THE WEIGHT OF PRAYERLESSNESS

In a recent survey, hundreds of people were asked to name the top three "weights" they felt were facing Christians in America today. Weight number six was unforgiveness.

When we refuse to forgive . . . when we choose, rather, to fetter ourselves with unforgiveness and drag that unwieldy weight around the racetrack with us, we are the ones who suffer.

In order to run and win the race God has set before us, we must learn what many great men and women of faith have learned: *forgiveness is a gift you give yourself.* This week, follow the Scripture diet and exercise program below to begin giving yourself the gift of forgiveness.

DAY 1

TODAY'S DIET: Romans 3:9-26; 10:9-10
EXERCISE: Think of a person who has forgiven you. What tangible benefits did you receive from that person? It might be flowers from a friend or spouse after a fight, an invitation to lunch after an argument with a co-worker, or a more unique form of forgiveness like receiving a warning instead of a ticket for a traffic violation. What other benefits (emotional, relational, spiritual, etc.) did you receive?

• Person who forgave me: _____

• Tangible benefit(s) I received: _____

• Intangible benefit(s) I received: _____

• Salvation is the ultimate forgiveness experience. Every individual ever born needs to be forgiven by God? Why? (See today's passage in Romans.)

• If you have never asked God to forgive you, He never has. You are still under a death penalty according to John 3:16-18. No forgiveness you will ever need or experience is as great as your need to ask God for His forgiveness.

What benefits do we receive when we are forgiven by God?

_____

_____

• When God saves us, *He* also benefits as the forgiver. He redeems — buys back — what He created. God created man so that man might fellowship with God and worship Him. When man sinned, that fellowship was broken. Man ran from God instead of wanting to be with Him.

But through the death and resurrection of Christ, the relationship between God and man is restored. Man benefits, and God, the forgiver benefits. So it is with every person who forgives: the forgiv*er* as well as the forgiv*en* benefit. Forgiveness is a gift we give ourselves.

DAY 2

TODAY'S DIET: Matthew 18:21-35
EXERCISE: Once we are saved, we are to grow, becoming more like God — more Christ-like — as time goes by. Copy Psalm 86:5 on the lines below.

_____

_____

_____

• Now, circle the qualities of God mentioned in the verse you just copied. To become more God-like and more Christ-like, those are the qualities we need to develop. Forgiveness is one of those qualities. Notice that God's forgiveness is both abundant and all-inclusive.

• Match each passage on the left with one of the brief synopses given on the right:

Let all bitterness, wrath, anger, clamor, and evil speaking be put away from you, with all malice. And be kind to one another, tenderhearted, forgiving one another, just as God in Christ also forgave you (Eph. 4:31-32).

• Be like God and forgive others.

Therefore, as the elect of God, holy and beloved, put on tender mercies, kindness, humbleness of mind, meekness, long-suffering; bearing with one another, and forgiving one another, if anyone has a complaint against another; even as Christ forgave you, so you also must do (Col. 3:12-13).

• Be like Christ and forgive others.

DAY 3

TODAY'S DIET: Hebrews 12:14,15; I Corinthians 6:1-8
EXERCISE: Today's passage in Hebrews warns about the "root of bitterness." Someone has said the *root* of bitterness always produces the *fruit* of bitterness. What might that fruit be?

_____

_____

• Unforgiveness generally spreads and involves other people. How was the lawsuit between believers in Corinth affecting other people? _____

_____

_____

• What was Paul's assessment of the situation? _____

_____

_____

• Did he think disputing believers would be effective witnesses? _____

• What solution did Paul suggest? _____

_____

DAY 4

TODAY'S DIET: Leviticus 19:17; I Timothy 3:1-5

EXERCISE: Forgiveness is not a fruit of the Spirit. It is a command that demands obedience. But obeying that command will be easier if the fruit of the Spirit is at work in our lives. Without that fruit and the help of the Holy Spirit, it is easy to wind up with just a form of godliness and no power to forgive.

• The fruit of the Spirit is like an orange with nine sections. List those sections from Galatians 5:22-23:

_____   _____

_____   _____

_____   _____

_____   _____

_____

• Think about how each "section" of the fruit of the Spirit is the opposite of unforgiveness; and about how each of those is necessary in order to be able to genuinely forgive someone.

• Read the three verses below. They are the verses that precede the "fruit of the Spirit verses." These verses list the works of the flesh. *Circle* each work of the flesh that could be the result of unforgiveness.

> Now the works of the flesh are evident, which are: adultery, fornication, uncleanness, licentiousness, idolatry, sorcery, hatred, contentions, jealousies, outbursts of wrath, selfish ambitions, dissensions, heresies, envy, murders, drunkenness, revelries, and the like; of which I tell you beforehand, just as I also told you in time past, that those who practice such things will not inherit the kingdom of God (Gal. 5:19-21).

• Now draw a *line* under each work of the flesh that could *contribute* to unforgiveness.

DAY 5

TODAY'S DIET: Galatians 6:1-3; Romans 12:14-20
EXERCISE: According to today's passage in Galatians, what kind of a person forgives? _____

_____

• After forgiving a person, according to the passage in Romans, we are to be ready to weep with that person when they're suffering . . . and ready to rejoice with them when they're being blessed. We are also to be their burden-bearer. In Romans 12:20, what "burdens" is the "enemy" bearing?

_____

• How are we to bear those burdens; i.e., what are we to do for him? _____

_____

_____

• Romans 12:20 and Proverbs 25:21-22 are nearly identical. Both say that meeting an enemy's needs is like heaping coals of fire on his head.

Although that sounds like a terrible thing to do, it is actually referring to a common, voluntary act of kindness.

In both Old and New Testament times, small stoves similar to modern-day barbecue grills were used for both cooking and heating purposes. A person who had run low on coals would often put a container on his head and walk through the neighborhood. As he passed beneath the second-story windows of neighbors, the more generous ones would reach out and place surplus coals in his container.

What modern-day equivalents of this act of kindness can you think of? _____

_____

_____

• Read the following verses. After reading the previous chapters and after following this week's diet and exercise program, tell in your own words what these verses mean to you.

> Then Peter came to Him and said, "Lord, how often shall my brother sin against me, and I forgive him? Up to seven times?" Jesus said to him, "I do not say to you, up to seven times, but up to seventy times seven" (Matt. 18:21-22).

_____

_____

_____

_____

28

THE HUBBLE WOBBLE

For the Scripture says . . .
"For this very purpose I have raised you up,
that I may show My power in you,
and that My name may be declared in all the earth."
— Romans 9:17

everal times a day, visitors to Cape Canaveral, Florida, tour the National Aeronautics and Space Administration facilities located there. A highlight of those tours includes a trip through the Mission Control Center which launched, monitored, and brought home the Apollo manned space missions.

During the tour, an actual countdown sequence is re-enacted with control panel lights activating as they did prior to each Apollo flight. Two of the lights illuminated include a red light labeled "Commit," and a green "Launch," light.

In the actual Apollo missions, the link between those two lights was vital — and short. Literally seconds. Because once the Commit light came on, Launch was imminent — and unstoppable. Lift-off could not be aborted. The "Commit-ment" had been made.

Each of the Apollo flights required months of preparation. Under President John F. Kennedy, America had made her own commitment — to manned space travel . . . to walking in space as well as on the moon — and through the Apollo project we fulfilled that commitment. Apollo made America proud.

Other space projects have not made us quite as proud — at least in the first go-round. The Hubble Telescope, carried into space aboard the Space Shuttle Discovery in April 1990, is a classic example.

Like Apollo, the Hubble also required months of preparation — a full year just to grind off 200 pounds of excess glass from the lens. Like Apollo, the Hubble was also designed for a purpose — to orbit 380 miles above the earth and transmit the clearest-ever pictures of distant space objects back to eagerly awaiting astronomers.

But the Hubble had a flaw in its optics — a two-micron error in the curvature of its main mirror. And that defect, less than the thickness of a single sheet of paper, prevented the Hubble for months from doing the kind of job it was created to do.

It was called a telescope. It even looked like a telescope. But until repaired, it didn't live up to our expectations. It wasn't giving us a good return on our $1.6 billion investment. It's just wasn't doing the job the way the job was supposed to be done.

But then, neither are many of us. And that became very clear in November 1992.

At that time, the governor of Mississippi, Kirk Fordice, spoke at a Republican governors' news conference. During his presentation, Governor Fordice made the "mistake" of saying:

> The United States of America is a Christian nation. The less we emphasize the Christian religion, the farther we fall into the abyss of poor character and chaos in the United States of America.

Within days, amidst a nationwide storm, Gov. Fordice apologized. November 23, the *Washington Times* observed,

> While most Americans are indeed Christian, their moral and ethical behavior and infrequent church attendance suggest a lack of Christian commitment.

Our theme verse is Hebrews 12:1:

> Let us lay aside every weight, and let us run with endurance the race that is set before us.

When hundreds of Christians were surveyed and asked to name the top three weights — burdens, cares, concerns, hindrances — that Christians face in America today, an overwhelming majority said that the Number One weight was "the lack of commitment." Another large percentage named the related matter of apathy.

It appears that as Christians, we, too, have developed a Hubble Wobble. We're *called* Christians. Most of us even *look like* Christians. But we're not living up to *our own* expectations, let alone God's! (After all, it was *us Christians* talking about *us Christians* in the survey!)

We said we're apathetic. *We* said we're not giving God the kind of return He deserves for His investment at Calvary. And *we said we're not doing the job the way the job is supposed to be done.*

Perhaps some of us don't even remember what the job is that we're supposed to be doing. Perhaps we've forgotten or never been taught exactly what Christian commitment involves. And if we don't know, how will new converts learn? They sure won't pick it up from our example — unless, that is, we carry out our own repair mission right here on earth!

In many churches of America, our expectations for commitment have sunk to an all-time low. We're so glad to have someone become a member, that we're scared to death to mention tithing or to suggest that they may have a role in ministry, for fear they'll *leave* the church the Sunday after they joined.

It's become so difficult to get long-term commitments for teachers of children's classes, that we don't dare suggest that someone actually attend quarterly leadership training, much less the worship service on Sunday morning.

Asking for people to come back to church on Sunday night — or to a business or committee meeting or a work day — is like requesting volunteers for martyrdom.

To expect anyone to actually get to know the person in the pew next to them . . . or to miss them when they're gone and actually find out why . . . or to fellowship with them in your home is automatic Twilight Zone!

We've moved into the McChurch mentality — each church competing with other spiritual retail outlets on other corners in the city. And the competition with other churches as well as with secular attractions requires that we cater to our "customers" rather than require commitment.

Instead of preaching responsibility and accountability, we've begun to stress peace of mind. Support instead of salvation and service. Help rather than holiness. And we've done it so long now, that both non-church members and church members have become, in society's thinking, spiritual equals; and the church has lost her role as the moral and religious standard of our culture.

The sad fact is, that generally speaking, the churches of America who demand the least have become the churches in the greatest demand. Meanwhile the churches — and church members — who still attempt to assert a position of moral and spiritual values are labeled "out of touch" at best; black-balled as the "radical religious right," at worst. And sadly, many of us have succumbed to the pressure, allowing our beliefs as the American church at large to be determined by majority vote or market surveys.

It's no wonder the *Washington Post* mused several

years ago that Christians lack commitment. And it's no wonder that former Governor Fordice apologized for even *suggesting* that we are a Christian nation.

We're not doing the job. For the most part, we've become self-centered, egotistical, and proud. Just plain fat and sassy. We've become spiritual couch potatoes.

The scary thing is that the Bible tells us that's exactly the shape Israel wound up in; and it was the downfall of their nation. Unless we lose the unsightly weight of apathy and disregard for the things of God, it may well be the downfall of ours as well.

Notice the link God placed on spiritual "fat" — the lack of commitment among His people — and the end of their joy and His blessing:

> Woe to you who put far off the day of doom, who cause the seat of violence to come near; who lie on beds of ivory, stretch out on your couches . . . who chant to the sound of stringed instruments, and invent for yourselves musical instruments like David; who drink wine from bowls, and anoint yourselves with the best ointments, but are not grieved for the affliction of Joseph (Amos 6:3-6).

> And [Israel] took strong cities and a rich land, and possessed houses full of all goods, cisterns already dug, vineyards, olive groves, and fruit trees in abundance. So they ate and were filled and grew fat, and delighted themselves in Your great goodness. Nevertheless they were disobedient and rebelled against You, cast Your law behind their backs (Neh. 9:25-26).

> For the Lord's portion is His people . . . . But Jeshurun [an honorable surname for Israel, meaning "righteous nation"] grew fat and

kicked; you grew fat, you grew thick, You are obese! Then he forsook God who made him, and scornfully esteemed the Rock of his salvation. . . . Of the Rock who begot you, you are unmindful, and have forgotten the God who fathered you (Deut. 32:9-18).

They have closed up their fat hearts; With their mouths they speak proudly. . . . Arise, O Lord, Confront him, cast him down (Ps. 17:10-13).

David the psalmist summed it up by saying that the committed delight in the law of God while the uncommitted have hearts *"as fat as grease"* (Ps. 119:70).

But what does all this mean for us today?

Two things. First of all, the dark clouds are gathering over our own nation. There's hardly a historian, politician, or statistician on the cutting edge of what's happening in America today who is not sounding an alarm — Christians and non-Christians alike. America is slipping — morally, economically, educationally, ethically.

The second factor is that throughout our history it has been the church of Jesus Christ who has brought America back online. When our morals became bad . . . when our character was less than it should have been . . . during economic downturns . . . environmental disasters . . . war . . . from slavery to civil rights, it has been the Church who stepped in and made the difference. It was the Church who led the way back to our historical foundations.

But the question now is, Will the Church rise to the occasion once again? *Can* she rise to the occasion? What will it take to get her — and us — back in shape . . . steady . . . focused . . . doing the job for which we were created?

The clues lie in the pages ahead. But are you committed enough to turn them and read?

Let us lay aside the weight of
the lack of commitment . . .
and let us run with endurance
the race that is set before us.
— based on Hebrews 12:1

29

THOU SHALT

Here is the patience of the saints;
here are those who keep the commandments of God
and the faith of Jesus.
— Revelation 14:12

Blessed are those
who do His commandments,
that they may have the right to the tree of life,
and may enter through the gates into the city.
— Revelation 22:14

Over and over again the New Testament tells us to keep the commandments — even though we are not under law, but under grace.
The apostle Paul said it to the church at Corinth:

> Circumcision is nothing and uncircumcision is nothing, but keeping the commandments of God is what matters (1 Cor. 7:19).

He said it again to the church at Thessalonica:

> Finally then, brethren, we urge and exhort in the Lord Jesus that you should abound more and more, just as you received from us how you

ought to walk and to please God; for you know what commandments we gave you through the Lord Jesus" (1 Thess. 4:1-2).

The apostle John said it:

> Now by this we know that we know Him, if we keep His commandments. He who says, "I know Him," and does not keep His commandments, is a liar, and the truth is not in him. But whoever keeps His word, truly the love of God is perfected in him. By this we know that we are in Him (1 John 2:3-5).

> And whatever we ask we receive from Him, because we keep His commandments and do those things that are pleasing in His sight. . . . Now he who keeps His commandments abides in Him, and He in him. And by this we know that He abides in us, by the Spirit whom He has given us (1 John 3:22-24).

> For this is the love of God, that we keep His commandments. And His commandments are not burdensome (1 John 5:3).

Even Jesus said it:

> If you want to enter into life, keep the commandments (Matt. 19:17).

> If you love Me, keep My commandments. . . . He who has My commandments and keeps them, it is he who loves Me. And he who loves Me will be loved by My Father, and I will love him and manifest Myself to him (John 14:15-21).

> If you keep My commandments, you will abide in My love, just as I have kept My Father's commandments and abide in His love. These

things I have spoken to you, that My joy may remain in you, and that your joy may be full (John 15:10-11).

But why would God emphasize commandment-keeping over and over again for Christians? We're the ones living in the "Church Age" . . . the "Age of Grace" . . . the time when the "law of liberty" abounds (James 2:25).

So why the emphasis on keeping God's commandments?

No doubt it's because God knew back then, when the New Testament was penned, that a day was coming when Christians running the race would be bogged down with things like frustration and unforgiveness, guilt and financial pressure and individualism . . . no time and little prayer.

As God looked ahead in time and saw us — a bunch of limping, lagging Christians, He noticed that many of us were looking around in bewilderment at how bad things have gotten and wondering why. And way back then, God even saw some of us filling out a survey, admitting that for the most part, across the board, we lack commitment.

So God inspired Matthew and Mark and Luke to specifically record in their Gospels the words of Jesus regarding obeying the commandments. And He inspired John and Paul to recap the subject in their letters to various groups of believers.

By focusing on what these men wrote under the inspiration of the Holy Spirit, we are forced to rethink the relationship between commandment-keeping and the matter of commitment. We are forced to admit that faith without works really is dead . . . that commitment without action is worthless (James 2:17-20). And we are prodded to discover that the commandments provide the guidelines for that kind of active commitment.

But what commands, exactly, are we to keep? That same question was asked some 2,000 years ago by a scribe.

Jesus was in Jerusalem, walking in the temple area.

As He walked, the religious leaders of the Jews approached Him, challenging Him with questions about where He got His authority . . . about whether Jews should pay Roman taxes . . . about marital status in the resurrection — questions all designed with entrapment in mind.

After successfully answering each, a scribe stepped forward, and asked:

> "Which is the first [or most important] commandment of all?"
>
> Jesus answered him, "The first of all the commandments is . . . You shall love the Lord your God with all your heart, with all your soul, with all your mind, and with all your strength." This is the first commandment.
>
> And the second, like it, is this: "You shall love your neighbor as yourself." There is no other commandment greater than these" (Mark 12:28-31).

Those are the commandments we are to keep. The ones that have to do with our commitment to God and others. Specifics are outlined in the New Testament. (We've already covered many in this book).

It's interesting to note that we sometimes speak of the salvation experience as "making a commitment to Christ." That commitment automatically involves loving God and loving others.

In the English language, the suffix, *"ee,"* is sometimes added to a verb to indicate a person involved in an action. An individual involved in a divorce is called a divorc*ee*. Someone involved in training is called a train*ee*. And a person actively employed by a company is called an employ*ee*.

So, then, would it be proper to say that someone who is involved in a commitment is a committ-*ee?* If that commitment is a commitment to Christ, it's exactly the right thing to say!

A committee is defined as a body of people appointed

to deal with particular matters. And when we are saved — when we make a commitment to Christ — we automatically become part of His body, according to Romans 12, and are accountable to and responsible for the other members in that body. We become a committ-*ee* — a member of that body, pledged to love God and others with all of our heart, mind, soul, and strength.

That means that our commitment to Christ should be greater . . . stronger . . . more consistent and dependable than our commitment to a sports team, for instance. It means that our commitment to Christ requires the same kind of responsibility we take for our families. And it means that commitment to Christ requires the same kind of accountability we demand — or are expected to give — on the job.

For instance, if your son or daughter didn't come home for weeks at a time, you'd file a missing person's report. But if a member of God's family misses weeks at church, do we care? Or follow up?

If your secretary didn't show up to take minutes during contract negotiations with an important client — if she said, "Oh, I didn't think *this* meeting was important" — you'd fire her. But how many times do we decide which meetings at church are important enough for us to attend?

You see, commitment requires some plain old hard work. The kind it takes to go to the Superbowl. Or to stay married 50 years. Or with the same job until retirement. It takes commitment. And consistency. But that's a subject for another chapter. . . .

---

*Let us lay aside the weight of
the lack of commitment . . .
and let us run with endurance
the race that is set before us.*
— based on Hebrews 12:1

30

A TRUE COMMITT-*EE*

Therefore, leaving the discussion
of the elementary principles of Christ,
let us go on to perfection. . . .
yes, things that accompany salvation. . . .
For God is not unjust to forget your work
and labor of love
which you have shown toward His name,
in that you have ministered to the saints, and do minister.
And we desire that each one of you
show the same diligence . . . until the end,
that you do not become sluggish,
but imitate those who through faith and patience
inherit the promises."
— Hebrews 6:1-12

It's clear that the practical meaning of commitment is something that's being virtually lost in almost every area of our lives.

If we can't meet our financial obligations, we refinance or consolidate our loans. And if all else fails, we file bankruptcy and get out of paying altogether.

If we don't want to be a brunette any longer, we can convert to a blonde in an hour — and a redhead tomorrow.

If we have an unpleasant task to perform, we can delegate it. Our word is only our bond if it's backed up in the fine print and even finer-tuned disclaimers.

The president speaks, then someone from his office comes out and tells us what he really "meant."

Contracts can be bought out or broken altogether.

Marriage vows are as fluid as the punch that flows at the reception.

And have you ever read these lines in everyday ads? "Prices may vary." "Subject to availability." "Actual size may be smaller than pictured."

No wonder the lack of commitment has crept into the church and believers' lives as well! But what exactly is commitment? *The New Lexicon Webster's Encyclopedic Dictionary of the English Language* defines it this way:

> (1) something which engages one to do something;
> (2) a continuing obligation;
> (3) the state of intellectual and emotional adherence to some political, social or religious theory or action or practice, especially the conscious linking of works . . . with such theory or action;
> (4) a promise, pledge.

Webster is saying that any way you figure it, commitment requires action — it's something which engages one to do something. It's an ongoing responsibility — a continuing obligation, and it involves your entire being; your intellect, your emotions, and your body are consciously linked to produce works that demonstrate or validate what you are committed to in theory or belief.

Jesus said it this way: Commitment involves your heart, your soul, your mind, and your strength. And there's no two ways about it, that kind of commitment involves a lot of plain old hard work.

Even the apostle Paul said that "work" is what being a Christian is all about:

> For we are His workmanship, created in Christ Jesus for good works, which God prepared beforehand that we should walk in them (Eph. 2:10).

> Jesus Christ . . . gave Himself for us, that He might redeem us . . . and purify for Himself His own special people, zealous for good works (Titus 2:13-14).

Physical work burns off physical fat. Spiritual work burns off spiritual fat. It trims down lazy, uncaring, uncommitted, "greasy" hearts and gets us back into spiritual shape.

"Works" also verify and validate commitment.

God's commitments to us are verified and validated by *His* works — what He has already done for us and what He continues to do for us. God planned before the creation of the world to send His Son, Jesus, to die for our sins (Rev. 13:8). The fact that He did it sealed His commitment to us.

When Jesus came to earth, He also demonstrated who He was and the level of *His* commitment by the *works* which He did. His *walk* matched His *talk.* Jesus said:

> The very works that I do — bear witness of Me, that the Father has sent Me (John 5:36).

In addition, Jesus indicated that He expects believers to not only be committed, but to demonstrate that commitment by their works:

> Most assuredly, I say to you, he who believes in Me, the works that I do he will do also; and greater works than these he will do, because I go to My Father (John 14:12).

After Jesus returned to heaven, those early followers did just that. Not only were they committed mentally and emotionally and spiritually, but their works — including many signs and wonders — verified and validated the commitment they had made to their risen Lord.

They prayed. They shared their resources, spiritual and physical. They traveled — even risked and lost their lives — to spread the gospel. The apostle Paul was one of those committ-*ees;* and he intended that the tradition continue:

> This is a faithful saying, and these things I want you to affirm constantly, that those who have believed in God should be careful to maintain good works. These things are good and profitable to men (Titus 3:8).

So what's the bottom line?

We admit we lack commitment. We know it's a weight that we need to lose. We understand that committing our lives to Christ requires action . . . that works verify and validate our witness. But exactly what kind of commitment are we talking about?

1. It's a co-commitment — with God and with others.

A committee — remember? And that's good news. We don't have to change the world — or even ourselves — alone.

There are many video exercise tapes on the market, and piece after piece of home exercise equipment is advertised each week in discount and sports store circulars. Yet the health and diet clubs of America flourish.

Why? Because it's a proven fact that people who join a group are more inspired to lose weight and shape up than are those who try to do it alone in their living rooms with Richard Simmons on tape.

Why? Because in a group there's camaraderie . . . there's responsibility . . . there's accountability . . . co-commitment. That's the power of the Church. And without that kind of co-commitment, the individual, the Church, and the nation suffer.

The apostle Paul wrote:

> For we are God's fellow workers (1 Cor. 3:9).

That's co-commitment to others ("we") and God, spelled out in six simple words. And notice, again, that we are not fellow spectators; we are fellow *workers*.

2. It's a caring, concerned commitment.

It's a family kind of commitment. As believers, we're called the children of God . . . the household of faith.

> Now, therefore, you are no longer strangers and foreigners, but fellow citizens with the saints and members of the household of God (Eph. 2:19).

It's a group of people who like to be together . . . who enjoy sharing their lives . . . and who take responsibility for the overall welfare of each other.

Paul set the example in his relationship with the believers in Thessalonica:

> But we were gentle among you, just as a nursing mother cherishes her own children. So, affectionately longing for you, we were pleased to impart to you not only the gospel of God, but also our own lives (1 Thess. 2:7-8).

Philipp Melanchton, who joined Martin Luther to lead the Reformation, put it this way:

> In essentials, unity; in nonessentials, liberty; in all things, charity.

3. It's a mutually challenging commitment.

It places some requirements on our time and our effort. It requires instruction and discipline. And it gives each believer responsibility toward other believers:

And He Himself gave some to be apostles, some prophets, some evangelists, and some pastors and teachers, for the equipping of the saints for the work of ministry, for the edifying of the body of Christ, till we all come to the unity of the faith and the knowledge of the Son of God, to a perfect man, to the measure of the stature of the fullness of Christ; that we should no longer be children, tossed to and fro and carried about with every wind of doctrine, by the trickery of men, in the cunning craftiness by which they lie in wait to deceive, but, speaking the truth in love, may grow up in all things into Him who is the head — Christ — from whom the whole body, joined and knit together by what every joint supplies, according to the effective working by which every part does its share, causes growth of the body for the edifying [building up] of itself in love (Eph. 4:11-16).

And let us consider one another in order to stir up love and good works, not forsaking the assembling of ourselves together, as is the manner of some, but exhorting one another, and so much the more as you see the Day [of Christ's return] approaching (Heb. 10:24-25).

And let our people also learn to maintain good works, to meet urgent needs, that they may not be unfruitful (Titus 3:14).

4. It's a recorded commitment.

The Scripture teaches that heaven has its own library, complete with the Book of Life, and volumes upon volumes detailing the deeds of mankind. One day those books will be opened and our commitment, or our lack of commitment, will be revealed by what we have — or have not — done.

And I saw the dead, small and great, standing before God, and books were opened. And another book was opened, which is the Book of Life. And the dead were judged according to their works, by the things which were written in the books. The sea gave up the dead who were in it, and Death and Hades delivered up the dead who were in them. And they were judged, each one according to his works (Rev. 20:12-13).

For we must all appear before the judgment seat of Christ, that each one may receive the things done in the body, according to what he has done, whether good or bad (2 Cor. 5:10).

5. It's a rewarded commitment.

Just as physical effort — diet and exercise — pays off in weight loss, toned muscles, firmed bodies, and healthier cardiovascular systems, so spiritual effort, or commitment, pays off — now as well as in eternity:

Blessed is the man Who walks not in the counsel of the ungodly, Nor stands in the path of sinners, Nor sits in the seat of the scornful;

But his delight is in the law of the Lord, And in His law he meditates day and night.

He shall be like a tree Planted by the rivers of water, That brings forth its fruit in its season, Whose leaf also shall not wither; And whatever he does shall prosper (Ps. 1:1-3).

And whatever you do, do it heartily, as to the Lord and not to men, knowing that from the Lord you will receive the reward of the inheritance; for you serve the Lord Christ (Col. 3:23-24).

Then I heard a voice from heaven saying to me, "Write: 'Blessed are the dead who die in the

Lord from now on.' " "Yes," says the Spirit, "that they may rest from their labors, and their works follow them" (Rev. 14:13).

Jesus said,

> Let your light so shine before men, that they may see your good works and glorify your Father in heaven (Matt. 5:16).

In other words, when others look at the mission control panel of your life, they ought to see the "Commit" light brightly lit; and they ought to see the "Launch" sequence rapidly progressing.

Our world desperately needs those who are empowered by the eternal engines of the Word and the Spirit of God . . . those who break free from the gravitational pull of an evil world . . . those who operate far above it . . . and who send back a clear, undistorted picture of what being a Christian and being a Christian nation is really all about. So where do we begin?

Each of us must personally affirm four truths:

Truth #1: A commitment must be made.

Unfortunately commitment does not happen without commitment.

Truth #2: I must make the commitment.

No one can do it for you. And you can't do it for anyone else. Your first commitment is to believe that Jesus Christ died on the cross and rose again to save you from your sins. And secondly, you must commit your life to Him.

Truth #3: My commitment as a Christian is to fulfill the Great Commission by carrying out the Great Commandments.

> Jesus said, "Go therefore and make disciples of all the nations, baptizing them in the name of the Father and of the Son and of the Holy Spirit,

teaching them to observe all things that I have commanded you; and lo, I am with you always, even to the end of the age" (Matt. 28:19-20).

The way to accomplish that is by loving God and others with everything we've got.

Truth #4: I *can* make the commitment.

You are a free moral agent. God has given you both the ability and the right to determine the level of your commitment. If it's been lacking lately, you can renew it with a simple prayer right now.

> Father,
> I ask You to forgive me
>   for not living up to Your expectations.
> Forgive me for not doing the job
>   that I am supposed to do as a Christian.
> I ask You to give me the courage to lay aside my apathy and become more committed to You
>   and others than I have ever been before.
> Help me to impact my world
>   and become an instrument of renaissance
>   and revival in America today.
> In Jesus' name I pray, Amen.

Let us lay aside the weight of unforgiveness . . .
and let us run with endurance
the race that is set before us.
— based on Hebrews 12:1

PART 10
LET US LAY ASIDE THE WEIGHT OF
THE LACK OF COMMITMENT

Hundreds of people were asked in a survey to name the top three "weights" they felt were facing Christians in America today. The number one weight named was "the lack of commitment." "Apathy," a related entity, was also frequently mentioned. Follow the Scripture diet and exercise program below to evaluate and improve the relationship with Christ and His church that you began when you made *your* commitment to Christ.

DAY 1

TODAY'S DIET: Romans 12

EXERCISE: *The New Lexicon Webster's Encyclopedic Dictionary of the English Language* defines "commitment" this way: (1) something which engages one to do something; (2) a continuing obligation; (3) the state of intellectual and emotional adherence to some political, social, or religious theory or action or practice, especially the conscious linking of works . . . with such theory or action; (4) a promise, pledge.

We sometimes speak of the salvation experience as "making a commitment" to Christ. In what ways do each of the definitions above explain what that commitment involves?

(1) _____

_____

(2) _____

_____

(3) _____

_____

(4) _____

_____

• In the English language, the suffix *ee* is sometimes added to a verb to indicate a person involved in an action — divorc*ee*, train*ee*, for example. But the word committ*ee* seems to be an exception, not indicating an *individual*, but a *group* of individuals. A *committee* is defined as "a body of people appointed or elected to examine or deal with particular matters."

When we make a commit*ment* to Christ, we automatically become part of His body, according to Romans 12, and are accountable to and responsible for the other members in that body, as well as to its head, the Lord Jesus Christ. How does this principle fit in with the idea of a Christian being a "committ-*ee?*" _____

_____

_____

• Why do you think commitment to Christ has become so shallow in our time? _____

_____

_____

• On a scale of 1 to 10, with 1 being *very low commitment* and 10 being *very high commitment,* how would you rate *your* commitment? (Circle the appropriate number.) Before beginning, re-read the previous definitions of commitment. And be sure to evaluate yourself in light of your relationship with the *whole* body of Christ, not just its *head!*

   1   2   3   4   5   6   7   8   9   10

DAY 2

TODAY'S DIET: Ephesians 2:19-22; 4:11-16
EXERCISE: Re-read the definition of *committee* in DAY 1. How does Ephesians 4:13 fit into that definition? ____

_____

_____

_____

• According to verse 14, what is one benefit of commitment? _____

_____

_____

• Is that an individual benefit, a corporate benefit, or both?

_____

_____

_____

• What is the additional benefit named in verse 15?_____

_____

_____

_____

• Is that an individual benefit, a corporate benefit, or both?

_____

_____

_____

• This passage has application, not only to the entire of body of Christ, but to local congregations as well. Evaluate the words and phrases in verse 16 as they relate to your commitment and involvement in your local church.

> From whom the whole body, joined and knit together by what every joint supplies, according to the effective working by which every part does its share, causes growth of the body for the edifying of itself in love (Eph. 4:16).

"the whole body joined and knit together"
   • Do you feel tied in to the rest of the congregation?
   • If not, why not?
   • Do you think others feel the same way you do?

"by what every joint supplies"
   • Joints indicate movement. What areas do you see your church moving to supply?

- Which ones are you actively committed to and involved in?
- What areas would you like to see your church move to supply?
- Are any of those areas ones you feel the Lord calling you into?

"effective working by which every part does its share"

- What do you feel is "your share" of the work your church does?
- Prayerfully consider how much of your time, resources, and energy you have devoted to "your share" of the work.

"causes growth of the body and the edifying of itself in love"

- This verse says that commitment to Christ involves evangelism (growth in the Body) and ministry (the edifying of itself in love). Active commitment to the body of Christ causes growth.
- Is your church growing?
- If not, could it be because its members are not actively committed?
- Could it be because *you* are not actively committed?

DAY 3

TODAY'S DIET: Amos 6:3-6; Hebrews 6:1-12

EXERCISE: Our survey respondents named "lack of commitment" as the number one weight hindering Christians in America today from effectively running the race God has set before us. Most of us agree: Christians in America today have become self-centered . . . egotistical. . . proud . . . just plain fat and sassy.

- Read Amos 6:3-6, noting some of the characteristics of spiritual couch potatoes. _____

_____

_____

_____

• Are you a spiritual couch potato? If so, you can start losing that "sluggishness" according to Hebrews 6:12 by "imitating those who through faith and patience inherit the promises." Select one of the heroes of the faith listed in Hebrews 11. Begin studying that person's life, and then imitate it.

DAY 4

TODAY'S DIET: Deuteronomy 32:9-18
EXERCISE: Carefully consider the following Scriptures:

> For the Lord's portion is His people. . . . But Jeshurun [a "nickname" for Israel] grew fat and kicked; you grew fat, you grew thick, you are covered with fat; then he forsook God who made him, and scornfully esteemed the Rock of his salvation. Of the Rock who begot you, you are unmindful, and have forgotten the God who fathered you (Deut. 32:9-18).

> They have closed up their fat hearts; With their mouths they speak proudly (Ps. 17:10).

> The proud have forged a lie against me, But I will keep Your precepts with my whole heart. Their heart is as fat as grease, But I delight in Your law (Ps. 119:69-70).

• Israel became proud and self-sufficient, and reneged on her commitment. Israel forgot the Rock of their salvation.

> Jesus said, "On this rock I will build My church, and the gates of Hell shall not prevail against it" (Matt. 16:18).

> And to His Church, Christ issued the Great Commission:

> All authority has been given to Me in heaven
> and on earth. Go therefore and make disciples of
> all the nations, baptizing them in the name of the
> Father and of the Son and of the Holy Spirit, teach-
> ing them to observe all things that I have com-
> manded you; and lo, I am with you always, even
> to the end of the age. Amen (Matt. 28:18-20).

The Great Commission requires Great Commitment. How
great is yours?

DAY 5

TODAY'S DIET: Luke 9:57-62
EXERCISE: Commitment is demonstrated by action.
God's commitment to us was demonstrated by His action
at Calvary: "But God demonstrates His own love toward
us, in that while we were still sinners, Christ died for us"
(Rom. 5:8).

• Our commitment to God is also to be demonstrated by
action: "For as the body without the spirit is dead, so faith
without works is dead also" (James 2:26).

• Read Acts 9:36. How did the disciple mentioned there
demonstrate her commitment? _____

_____

_____

• Read Titus 3:8. What did Paul say "those who have believed in God" should be careful to maintain? Why? _____

_____

_____

• Describe the kind of commitment Paul had toward other
believers. See 1 Thessalonians 2:7-8. _____

_____

_____

• Paul longed to be with other believers. What, besides the

gospel, did he feel was important to share with them?___

_____

_____

• Commitment to Christ and His church is a mutually challenging commitment, requiring accountability to each other and time together. Read Hebrews 10:24-25 and evaluate your commitment in the light of those verses.

• According to Titus 3:14, commitment requires instruction and discipline; and commitment meets needs.

• When you say, "I'll pray for you," do you?

• When you say, "Let me know if there's anything I can do," do you secretly hope that person will never call?

• Do you "do" something even if that person doesn't call?

AN EXTRA-CHALLENGE ASSIGNMENT

Read the following verses (the messages to the seven churches in the Book of Revelation). Find the phrase having to do with commitment, that is common to each (the same phrase is found in all seven passages).

> Revelation 2:1-2 — to the church at Ephesus
> Revelation 2:8-9 — to the church at Smyrna
> Revelation 2:12-13 — to the church at Pergamos
> Revelation 2:18-19 — to the church at Thyatira
> Revelation 3:1-2 — to the church at Sardis
> Revelation 3:7-8 — to the church at Philadelphia
> Revelation 3:14,15 — to the church at Laodicea

> Then I heard a voice from heaven saying to me, "Write: 'Blessed are the dead who die in the Lord from now on.'" "Yes," says the Spirit, "that they may rest from their labors, and their works follow them" (Rev. 14:13).

31

SUCCESS BY THE BOOK

*"For My thoughts are not your thoughts,
nor are your ways My ways," says the Lord.
"For as the heavens are higher than the earth,
so are My ways higher than your ways,
and My thoughts than your thoughts."*
— Isaiah 55:8-9

D r. Robert Schuller often asks seminar attendees, "What would you do if you knew you could not fail?" When hundreds of Christians were asked to name things that were weighting them down and holding them back from living successful, prosperous lives, the fear of failure ranked number ten. Not failure itself, but the *fear* of failure.

That seems strange at first glance, because of all people, Christians should be fear-free. Of all people, Christians should have faith in their ability, through the power of God, to achieve . . . to succeed . . . to prosper . . . and experience the joy of the Lord while doing it.

After all, the apostle Paul, speaking for all blood-bought believers said,

> I can do all things through Christ who strengthens me (Phil. 4:13).

Don't we have that same Christ today? And isn't He still able to strengthen us as He strengthened the apostle Paul?

We know that God desires that His people succeed. And He longs to equip us to achieve that success. Psalm 35:27 says,

> Let the Lord be magnified, Who has pleasure in the prosperity of His servant.

Second Corinthians 2:14 says,

> Now thanks be to God who always leads us in triumph in Christ.

Yet, according to our survey, many Christians today are willing to openly admit that they're not at all convinced that they will always triumph. They fact is, many of us are very much afraid that we're going to fail.

But what, exactly, is failure — this thing that so many of us fear? *Webster's Encyclopedic Dictionary* says that failure is "the lack of success."

Well then, what is success?

Jesus told a group of 11 men — disciples — to go into all the world and preach the gospel. Yet not one of them made it to America. Were those 11 disciples successful? Or were they failures?

At Caesarea Philippi, Jesus said to His disciples:

> I will build my church and the gates of death [or the gates of failure] shall not prevail against it (Matt. 16:18).

Jesus was really saying that His church was going to be victorious. "No matter what the devil throws at My church," Jesus said, "My church is going to be successful."

And you know the story. The fire fell on the Day of Pentecost . . . power came . . . and thousands were added to that first church at Jerusalem. Those early Christians believed what Jesus had told them — that He was coming back — and they thought He meant right away. So they sold everything they owned, and became some of the most bold witnesses for Christ that history has ever seen. And from that church at Jerusalem, missionaries were sent out to establish churches in every corner of the then-known world.

Until they ran out of money, that is. Until they had used up everything they owned in ministry. Until the church at Jerusalem was broke and the other missionary churches had to send back relief.

So, was the church a failure? Or a success?

If you look at Hebrews 11, called "Faith's Hall of Fame," you read about great men and women of the Bible: Abel, Enoch, Noah, Abraham and Sarah, Isaac, Jacob, Joseph, Moses, Joshua, Rahab, Gideon, Samson, David, Samuel, the prophets. But when you come to the end of the chapter, verse 39, you read:

> And all these, having obtained a good testi-
> mony through faith, did not receive the promise
> (Heb. 11:39).

These were the men and women of faith who performed great exploits for God; yet, the Bible says, none of them have yet received the promise God made to them.

And if you look just a few verses prior, the martyrs are listed — people who were tortured, mocked, scourged, chained, imprisoned, stoned, sawn in two, beheaded, left homeless — all for the cause of Christ.

So, would you say that these MVPs in the Hebrews 11 Hall of Faith failed? Or did they succeed?

Whether something or someone is deemed a "failure" (or a "success") depends on two things:

1. what standards of measurement are used; and
2. who's doing the measuring.

The problem many of us have run into is that we have allowed the "fear of failure" to become a weight because we are allowing ourselves to be judged by the wrong set of standards; and/or we are letting the wrong person or people do the measuring.

As we've already seen from passages like Psalm 35:27 and 2 Corinthians 2:14, God never intended for His people to fail. But He also never intended that every single believer be an absolute and total success *by the world's standards.*

God judges our failure or success by *His* standards — not by ours.

Sometimes the two standards — the world's and God's — look pretty much alike. For instance, the world at large frowns on things like violence, corruption, murder, robbery, extortion, etc. So does God.

But more often, the two sets of standards disagree; and sometimes they are exact opposites.

For instance, by the world's standards, Jesus was a financial failure. After 33 years, He didn't even have a place to lay His head (Luke 9:58).

By the world's standards, Peter was irresponsible. One day Jesus came by, invited Peter to follow Him, and Peter just walked off, leaving a boat and all the nets sitting on the dock (Matt. 4:18-20).

By the standards of the world, John the Baptist was a failure. He could have had one of the largest followings ever; but he had a fatalistic attitude when it came to his cousin, Jesus. John said, "He must increase and I must decrease," and sent his own disciples and the crowds that were following him to follow Jesus instead (John 3:30).

Any social worker worth her salt would declare Hannah one of the worst mothers of all time. You remember Hannah from the Old Testament. She prayed for a child . . . God answered her prayer . . . and what did she do? She took her little boy, Samuel, when he was just a preschooler, and left him in the care of an old priest at the temple. And to top it all off, she only visited him after that once a year. A pretty poor example of motherhood, the world would say.

Jesus. Peter. John the Baptist. Hannah. All were failures by one set of standards; but chosen servants of God by another.

The lesson we can learn from them is that the first step we must take to overcome the fear of failure is to define for ourselves what success is and what failure — or the lack of that success — really is.

We must decide:

(1) which standard of measurement we will apply — the world's or God's,
(2) we must decide who we will allow to apply that standard of measurement.

Will we listen to the world and build our lives in accordance with its standards? Or will we listen to the voice and Word of God?

Because success for the Christian is finding the will of God as revealed in the Word of God, and then doing that will of God by the power of God for the glory of God.

Simply put, finding the will of God as revealed in the Word of God means that we have to search the Scriptures to see what is best for us from God's point of view. We have to listen for His voice in our quiet times with Him. We are His creation, and as His creation, He has the best in mind for us — in our personal lives, our professional lives, in our relationships with each other, in our finances — in every single area of our lives. Once we discover God's best for us, it is then up to us to claim His strength — "I can do all things through Christ" — to achieve His will in our lives for His glory. And that involves taking on failure's formidable companion called "fear," a topic you'll discover on the following pages.

Let us lay aside the weight of the fear of failure . . .
and let us run with endurance
the race that is set before us.
— based on Hebrews 12:1

32

FEAR SOME

Thus says the Lord:
"Let not the wise man glory in his wisdom,
let not the mighty man glory in his might,
nor let the rich man glory in his riches;
but let him who glories glory in this,
that he understands and knows Me,
that I am the Lord,
exercising lovingkindness, judgment,
and righteousness in the earth.
For in these I delight," says the Lord.
— Jeremiah 9:23-24

One of the intriguing parts of the survey was that Christians were not dragging around a weight of failure, but rather, a weight of the *fear* of failure. The next step in shedding this undue, burdensome weight, then, is to develop a healthy respect for fear.

Fear in itself is not bad. It is a God-given emotional reflex designed to warn us of danger, and motivate us to do something when necessity arises.

Fear prepares us for action. It increases the flow of adrenaline, makes us more alert, and increases the oxygen and energy available to our minds and muscles. Fear, like love, is a motivator; it gets us to move — to do something about whatever we're afraid of.

But when we allow fear to paralyze us . . . to stop us in our tracks or in the middle of the race that God has set before us . . . we wind up groveling in the emotion of fear itself. We kill its motivational impetus and begin the unhealthy mental and emotional pattern of continual worry and constant anxiety.

Fear and being afraid can become habitual . . . and the effects are devastating. Christians who allow the fear of failure to become a weight are, without exception, inactive and ineffective. The only thing they succeed at is failure . . . after failure . . . after failure.

But Christians who respect the fear of failure as the motivational force God intended it to be, accept the challenge, and will, without exception, become *more active* than they've been before and *more effective* than they've ever been.

The question is, how do we appropriate the potential strength inherent in the fear of failure?

The answer lies in the truth that we must fear some; i.e., we must have some fear of failure — at least to the degree that we acknowledge our inability to succeed in our own strength alone. To have no fear of failure and total confidence in our own human ability is a proud and dangerous condition.

The Bible indicates that if God prioritizes sin, then pride is Number One on His hit list. Because pride is a sense of self-sufficiency and self-exaltation.

Satan, or Lucifer as he was called at first, was expelled from heaven because of pride. "I will exalt my throne," he said, "above the stars of God" (Isa. 14:13). His attitude and actions stood in direct opposition to the standards of God.

Three times, Jesus used the same text for the same sermon in different locations:

Whoever exalts [honors, elevates, applauds] himself will be abased [demoted, humiliated], and he who humbles himself will be exalted (Matt. 23:12; Luke 14:11; 18:14).

The standards of the world encourage us to be like the prince of this world, Satan, and to exalt ourselves . . . to become self-sufficient — or to at least appear that way. We are challenged to develop our mind power, our will power, and our own abilities — and to rely on them exclusively.

But as believers and followers of Jesus Christ, God wants us to operate according to His standards. It requires a new mindset according to Romans 12:2 that enables us to recognize the new goals that are set before us. We have a new Master . . . a new purpose . . . a new, eternal time frame that must be brought in view. In other words, personal pride must be exchanged for personal humility, probably the Number One virtue in God's economy.

Humility is not timidity. Rather, humility is dependence — dependence upon God. Humility is marked by a healthy fear of failure. It's admitting that without God, you may succeed as far as the world's standards are concerned, but then again you may not. And for certain, you will fail and fall in the particular race that God has set before you.

A healthy fear of failure agrees that:

Without Him, we can do nothing (John 15:5).

A healthy fear of failure acknowledges that:

The things which are impossible with men are possible with God (Luke 18:27).

And a healthy fear of failure humbly admits weakness, opening the door to the empowering, enabling strength of Almighty God and, therefore, success, by His standards:

My strength [God's strength] is made perfect in weakness (2 Cor. 12:9).

Since fear was designed by God as a powerful motivator, it stands to reason that a healthy fear of failure will provide the required spiritual motivation that we need to run the race God has set before us — and to succeed in winning it.

But an unhealthy fear of failure — pride in our own ability — becomes a burdensome, constant weight of worry and anxiety, because we are forced to depend upon our own inadequate human resources for success.

Unfortunately, even the right kind — the healthy kind of fear of failure can become sick. It can even die. In fact, it will flat-line any time humility is smothered by pride. The spiritual morgue drawers are full of the victims of pride, but perhaps the classic scriptural example is found in the life of Saul, the first king of Israel.

God told Saul to lead the armies of Israel against the Amalekites. And while God guaranteed victory, He prohibited the taking of any captives or booty. Saul disobeyed and spared the king; and when he saw all the livestock the Amalekites had, he just couldn't bring himself to utterly destroy all the plump sheep and fat cattle.

By the world's standards, it just didn't make sense.

At that moment, Saul's spiritual heart monitor began beeping wildly. Saul never heard it. But the preacher Samuel did — right along with the bleating of the sheep and the lowing of the cows.

When Samuel asked Saul what was going on, Saul outlined a terrific proposal. Maybe it was his plan all along; or maybe it was just one he made up when Samuel put him on the spot.

Either way, by the world's standards, it sounded like a good idea. "The people," Saul said, "spared all the best sheep and cattle to sacrifice to God."

God liked sacrifices, right? God would be pleased that they were giving Him the best of the livestock, right? Wrong. God's standards had been violated. God wanted obedience, not plump sheep and fat cows. And it was soon clear that God didn't want a greasy-hearted, overweight, self-sufficient, proud king either. Samuel said,

> When you were little in your own eyes, were you not head of the tribes of Israel? And did not the Lord anoint you king over Israel? . . .
>
> Has the Lord as great delight in burnt offerings and sacrifices, as in obeying the voice of the Lord? Behold, to obey is better than sacrifice, and to heed than the fat of rams.
>
> For rebellion is as the sin of witchcraft, and stubbornness is as iniquity and idolatry. Because you have rejected the word of the Lord, He also has rejected you from being king (1 Sam. 15:17-23).

Saul lost it all because he allowed his humility and his healthy sense of the fear of failure — his dependence on God — to perish in the stranglehold of pride.

Take a moment to evaluate the level of your fear of failure. If you have none, you may need to exercise some pride. If you have too much — if you really do experience times when you are afraid you may fail, the next chapter holds a special message just for you.

Let us lay aside the weight of the fear of failure . . .
and let us run with endurance
the race that is set before us.
—based on Hebrews 12:1

33

THROUGH THE VIEWFINDER

The fear of man brings a snare,
but whoever trusts in the Lord shall be safe.
— Proverbs 29:25

He Himself has said,
"I will never leave you nor forsake you."
So we may boldly say:
"The Lord is my helper; I will not fear.
What can man do to me?"
— Hebrews 13:5-6

The fear of failure is a two-sided coin. On the one side there is "healthy" fear — the kind that involves humility and dependence on God. But on the other side of that shiny coin there is a tarnished version of fear — an unhealthy sense of apprehension and anxiety, dread and dismay. A person who constantly lugs around this kind of weighty fear is generally known as a worrier and is often stressed-out, sometimes to the point of near panic.

And let's admit it, we all have our moments when we doubt whether we'll ever succeed . . . when we're unsure that we're really doing what we ought to be doing . . . when we are almost certain that we're going to fail.

So how do we keep from flat-lining as Saul did? By taking some important steps the minute we hear the first beep from our spiritual heart monitor:

1. Re-focus.

Too many times, this weight we call "the fear of failure" is really the fear of being *viewed* as a failure.

We're not really as afraid of financial failure as we are of being *viewed* as a financial failure . . . like when we can't buy the new car . . . or when we don't have the latest model of video camera . . . or when we can't entertain or dress or live as lavishly as some others do. We're not really as afraid of being a failure as a parent as we are of being *viewed* as a failure when our children embarrass us.

This fear of being viewed as a failure is what prompted God to issue a stern command when His people moved into the Promised Land. God said,

> You shall not seek their peace nor their prosperity all your days forever (Deut. 23:6).

What the Canaanites would call peace and prosperity — treaties and compromise — was not the same as what God called peace and prosperity. So God said, "Don't adopt the world's set of standards. And don't worry about how other people view your version of peace and prosperity. Just stick to my standards, and you'll never go wrong."

Years later Ezra, the priest, repeated the same principle to the people returning to the Promised Land from captivity. Ezra said,

> The land which you are entering to possess is an unclean land, with the uncleanness of the peoples of the lands, with their abominations which have filled it from one end to another with their impurity. Now therefore . . . never seek their peace or prosperity, that you may be strong and

eat the good of the land, and leave it as an inheritance to your children forever (Ezra 9:11-12).

Even John the Apostle, under the inspiration of the Holy Spirit, was compelled to warn us to re-focus occasionally . . . to re-evaluate our own personal sense of success or failure . . . and to determine whether we are measuring ourselves by the standards of the world or by the standards of God:

> Do not love the world or the things in the world. If anyone loves the world, the love of the Father is not in him. For all that is in the world — the lust of the flesh, the lust of the eyes, and the pride of life — is not of the Father but is of the world. And the world is passing away, and the lust of it; but he who does the will of God abides forever (1 John 2:15-17).

2. Don't hang around others who are weighed down with the fear of failure.

That principle is played out graphically in an account recorded in Deuteronomy 20:

> When you go out to battle against your enemies, and see horses and chariots and people more numerous than you, do not be afraid of them; for the Lord your God is with you, who brought you up from the land of Egypt.
>
> So it shall be, when you are on the verge of battle, that the priest shall approach and speak to the people.
>
> And he shall say to them, "Hear, O Israel: Today you are on the verge of battle with your enemies; do not let your heart faint, do not be afraid, and do not tremble or be terrified because of them; for the Lord your God is He who goes with you, to fight for you against your

enemies, to save you." . . .

Then the officers shall speak further to the people, and say, "What man is there who is fearful and fainthearted? Let him go and return to his house, lest the heart of his brethren faint like his heart" (Deut. 20:1-8).

Let us lay aside the weight of the fear of failure . . .
and let us run with endurance
the race that is set before us.
— based on Hebrews 12:1

PART 11
LET US LAY ASIDE THE WEIGHT OF
THE FEAR OF FAILURE

In a survey, Christians named the fear of failure — but not failure itself — as a weight they believe keeps many people from living happy and successful lives. Use the following diet and exercise plan to evaluate your definition of success, as well as your current level of fear with regard to failure.

DAY 1

TODAY'S DIET: Philippians 4:4-13

EXERCISE: Many believers memorize Philippians 4:13 — "I can do all things through Christ who strengthens me" — but fail to really put it into practice in their lives. Why do you think that is?

Do you think it has more to do with our view of God, or our view of ourselves? Explain your answer. _____

_____

_____

_____

Do you think our failure to put Philippians 4:13 at work in our lives has anything to do with the kinds of things we are attempting to do? Why or why not? _____

_____

_____

_____

Do you think it could be because we don't really know how to tap into the strength of Christ? _____

_____

_____

_____

• What do each of the following verses teach us about strength and success or failure?

The joy of the Lord is your strength (Neh. 8:10). _____

_____

_____

The way of the Lord is strength for the upright, but destruction will come to the workers of iniquity (Prov. 10:29). _____

_____

_____

Trust in the Lord forever, for in the Lord, is everlasting strength (Isa. 26:4). _____

_____

_____

In quietness and confidence shall be your strength (Isa. 30:15). _____

_____

_____

"Not by might nor by power, but by My Spirit," says the Lord of hosts (Zech. 4:6). ___

_____

_____

DAY 2

TODAY'S DIET: Philippians 3:3-10
EXERCISE: The apostle Paul wrote of himself that if anyone was a success from the world's point of view, he was. After reading the Philippians passage, list some of Paul's earthly (or "fleshly") achievements.

_____

_____

_____

_____

_____

_____

• What value did Paul say he placed on them? _____
_____
_____

• Do you think Paul thought his worldly achievements were bad? Why or why not? _____
_____

• Were any of them good as far as his ministry was concerned? _____
_____
_____

• Do you think God frowns on earthly success? Why or why not? Consider 3 John 1:2 in your answer. _____
_____
_____

• List some of your earthly (or "fleshly" achievements):
_____
_____
_____
_____

• Do you place the same kind of value on them that Paul did?

• Which of them are you currently using to serve the Lord? Which of them *could* be used to serve the Lord?

DAY 3

TODAY'S DIET: Matthew 27:11-50

EXERCISE: Successful Christians, from God's point of view, are believers who have learned to depend on God rather than in their own strength and abilities. Jesus set the example for us by modeling this kind of humble relationship. Rewrite what Jesus said in the following verses to describe the kind of dependent relationship you would like to have with the Heavenly Father:

Most assuredly, I say to you, the Son can do nothing of Himself, but what He sees the Father do; for whatever He does, the Son also does in like manner (John 5:19).

_____

_____

_____

I can of Myself do nothing. As I hear, I judge; and My judgment is righteous, because I do not seek My own will but the will of the Father who sent Me (John 5:30).

_____

_____

_____

Then Jesus said to them, "When you lift up the Son of Man, then you will know that I am He, and that I do nothing of Myself; but as My Father taught Me, I speak these things" (John 8:28).

_____

_____

_____

• Each of the following accounts describes an incident in the life of Jesus. Mark each, indicating whether you believe it was a success or a failure from the world's point of view. Then mark each, indicating whether you believe the occurrence was a success or a failure from God's point of view.

	World's Standards		God's Standards	
	success	not a success	success	not a success
Matt. 27:42				
John 12:12-13				
Mark 2:16-17				
John 11:20-21				
Matt. 14:13-20				
Luke 5:4-8				

• What did you learn from the previous exercise? _____

_____

_____

_____

DAY 4

TODAY'S DIET: Judges 6:11-16; 7:1-22

EXERCISE: When the Angel of the Lord appeared to Gideon, Gideon was hiding, threshing wheat in a winepress to keep it safe from an oppressive enemy. Even though Gideon was hiding, how did the angel address him? _____

_____

• What does this tell us about how God views our chances of success? _____

_____

_____

• What does it tell us about how *we* often view those same chances? _____

_____

_____

• God guaranteed that Gideon would lead Israel in a victory over the Midianites. What was Gideon's reaction? Would you agree that he feared failure? _____

_____

_____

• What did God say would be the deciding factor in the victory? _____

_____

_____

• Are you hiding from some particular "enemy?" Do you feel inadequate to defeat that enemy? What does Gideon's story teach you about the fear of failure and success? ___

_____

_____

• In chapter seven, Gideon musters an army of 32,000. Of those, how many feared failure at the hands of the enemy?

_____

_____

• That amounts to slightly more than a 2/3 majority. Would you say that is more than, about the same as or less than the number of Christians you know who are afraid of failing?

_____

_____

• Why did God say that He wanted a small army — eventually an army of only 300 — to go up against the enemy?

_____

_____

• What might God be saying to you through that same verse?

_____

_____

DAY 5

TODAY'S DIET: Psalm 56

EXERCISE: Many times the fear of failure tries to overwhelm us as we begin a new venture in life — a new job, going to college, getting married, starting a family, volunteering to help with a church or community project, etc. The Bible outlines a basic attack plan for controlling the fear of failure and turning it into the motivating factor for success that God intended it to be. (And by the way, this plan works for old ventures as well as new ones!)

Read the following verses, then fill in the blanks to outline that plan.

Commit your way to the Lord, Trust also in Him, And He shall bring it to pass (Ps. 37:5).

Commit your works to the Lord, and your thoughts will be established (Prov. 16:3).

1. C_____ the project to the Lord.
2. T_____ in God — not yourself — to bring the project to a successful conclusion.
3. Believe that God will e_____ your thoughts.

• When God "establishes" your thoughts, it is as though He installs new software in your mind that becomes an operating system in your life. That system is described in 2 Timothy 1:7. As a result of God establishing our thoughts — or installing new "thought" software — what kind of "program" will we be operating under?

> For God has not given us a spirit of fear, but of power and of love and of a sound mind (2 Tim. 1:7).

It is a program of p_____.
It is a program of l_____.
And it is the program of a s_____
    m_____.

• What element is completely foreign to the program?

The s_____ of f_____.

• Under the Psalm 37:5 / Proverbs 16:3 / 2 Timothy 1:7 program, would you be more likely to fear failure? Or expect success? Would you be more likely to achieve failure or success?

• In Isaiah 41:10, God tells us to not be afraid, and He gives five reasons why. What are they?

> Fear not, for I am with you; be not dismayed, for I am your God. I will strengthen you, yes, I will help you, I will uphold you with My righteous right hand.

1. Because _____

2. Because _____

3. Because _____

4. Because _____

5. Because _____

• Which of those reasons is most meaningful to you at this time? Why?

• **Remember that any weight loss program requires commitment and consistency. Review these materials often to stay in shape, to run the race, and win!**